Published in the Isle of Man by Lily Publications Ltd, PO Box 33, Ramsey, Isle of Man IM99 4LP
Copyright © 2017 Lily Publications Ltd. All rights reserved.
ISBN 978-1-911177-24-1
The right of Alan Cooper to be identified as the author of this work has been asserted in accordance with the
Copyright Act 1991.

No part of this publication may be reproduced, stored in a retrieval system or transmitted in any form or by any
means, electronic, mechanical, photocopying, recording or otherwise, without prior permission in writing from
the publisher.

Tel: +44 (0) 1624 898446 · Fax: +44 (0) 1624 898449 · www.lilypublications.co.uk · lilypubs@manx.net

SHORT WALKS TO HIDDEN GEMS

Map No.	Place	Description	Terrain	Miles	OS map reference	Restricted mobility
1	Ayres Nature Reserve	Low-lying heathland and sand dune coastline, paradise for birdwatchers, Area of Special Scientific Interest	Easy	½-2	438038	Y
2	Bride and Point of Ayre	Churchyard with Sir Norman Wisdom's grave; expansive beach and lighthouses on tip of the Island	Easy	½	449012	Y
3	Elfin Glen and Albert Tower	Woodland walk between two famous TT landmarks, separate path to Albert Tower, great views of Ramsey and the north	Moderate to steep	2	449934	
4	Ballure Reservoir and Glen	Woodland walk down to and round to a delightful little reservoir, option of walk down glen to the beach	Easy to moderate	¾-1½	453930	
5	Port e Vullen	Walk along low cliffs and beach, stroll through picturesque hamlet with unique phone box	Easy	1	470929	
6	Maughold Church and Head	Historic church, carved Viking stones, walk in tranquil setting	Easy	¾	493917	Y
7	Ballafayle	Grassland walk to monuments both ancient and modern, stunning coastal views: easy ½ mile	Easy	½	478901	Y
8	Ballaglas Glen	Idyllic glen walk following the spectacular Cornaa river, numerous waterfalls	Easy to moderate	1-1½	468898	
9	Cashtal yn Ard	Well preserved monument nearly as old as Stonehenge, commanding hill and coastal views	Easy	½	462892	Y
10	Port Cornaa	Beach, river and woodland walk, an opportunity to paddle in salt and fresh water	Easy	¾	473879	
11	Dhoon Glen	Magnificent glen, spectacular waterfall, original art forms on the beach	Steep in places	1½	453864	
12	Tholt-y-Will Glen	Woodland walk, steepling views down Sulby valley, delightful waterfall	Easy to moderate	1½	378897	
13	Sulby Reservoir	Walk round Island's largest reservoir in rugged upland countryside	Easy	1	374890	Y
14	Snaefell	The Island's only mountain (just) with immense panoramic views of the 7 Kingdoms	Moderate to steep	2	389859	
15	Beinn y Phott	Relatively easy short walk to summit with panoramic views stretching over a dozen miles	Easy to moderate	¾	389859	
16	Agneash	Tranquil upland valley looking towards Snaefell, historic mining site	Easy to moderate	2	431861	
17	King Orry's Grave, Laxey	Famous pre-historic monument, bi-sected by politician's home	Easy	¼	438843	Y
18	Laxey Glen Gardens	Picturesque glen walk through a former pleasure garden	Easy	1	431843	Y
19	Windy Corner	The shortest walk to a significant hill summit, panoramic views of Douglas and Laxey	Moderate	½	391845	
20	Kerrowdhoo and Clypse Reservoirs	Walk round two picturesque reservoirs on the edge of countryside	Easy	1	400807	Y
21	Lonan Old Church	Small historic church in remote setting, 1500 year old Celtic Cross	Easy	¼	427784	Y
22	Groudle Glen	Coast and glen walk, with several delights including steam railway, waterwheel and a wizard	Easy	1	420784	
23	Onchan Wetlands	Small but perfectly formed and peaceful nature reserve in centre of old Onchan village	Easy	¼	400782	Y
24	Port Jack Glen	Peaceful and attractive park, walk by stream	Easy	½	399773	Y
25	Summerhill Glen floodlit at night	Woodland walk by river with many curiosities, Easy to moderate	¾		394775	
26	Millennium Oakwood	Stroll round commemorative wood in a picturesque setting, Sword of State monument	Easy	¾	365779	Y
27	Braaid	Well preserved Iron Age and Viking homesteads in open countryside	Easy	½	325765	
28	Marine Drive	Dramatic cliff top views, follows course of former railway	Easy	1½-2½	382742	Y
29	Real Fairy Bridge	Countryside walk to secret place of folklore interest	Easy	1	357748	
30	Port Soderick	Woodland walk by rushing stream, secluded scenic bay	Easy	½	346726	Y
31	Arragon House	Woodland and stream walk around grounds of a mansion, riot of colour in spring, an ostentation of peacocks	Easy	½	316705	Y
32	Silverdale Glen	Woodland walk by babbling stream feeding in to duck pond, historic merry-go-round: additional walk to historic pack-horse bridge	Easy	1-2¼	275710	

SHORT WALKS TO HIDDEN GEMS

Map No.	Place	Description	Terrain	Miles	OS map reference	Restricted mobility
33	St Michael's Isle	Undisturbed islet with historic chapel and fort, reached by causeway	Easy	½	294674	Y
34	Langness	Coast and heathland walk, very varied scenery in such a short walk	Easy	1-1½	285660	Y
35	Scarlett Point	Varied coastline walk with several places of special note, remains of limestone quarrying	Easy	1	258666	
36	Balladoole, Castletown	Impressive Viking burial on site with expansive coastal and inland views, lake in disused quarry	Easy	½	246682	Y
37	Sugarloaf and Anvil	Countryside and cliff walk, Island's most dramatic coastline feature	Easy to moderate	1¾	202675	
38	Sound and the Calf of Man	Island's most renowned beauty spot, coastal stroll and views to Calf of Man	Easy	½	173667	Y
39	Meayll Circle, Cregneash	Well-preserved 5,000 year old ceremonial site with views over to the Calf of Man	Easy	½	189679	Y
40	Bradda Glen	Clifftop path round bay of Victorian seaside resort	Easy	½	195697	Y
41	Bradda Head and Milner's Tower	Glen walk with climb over open grassland to famous landmark with spectacular sea cliff views	Easy to moderate	1½	195697	
42	Colby Glen and Ballakilpheric	Tranquil wooded glen following the river, option of countryside walk to old hamlet	Easy	½-2	232709	
43	Earystane Nature Reserve, Colby	Stroll through woodland and curragh wetland, a hide for birdwatching	Easy	½	235715	Y
44	Cringle Reservoir	Walk round reservoir adjoining woodland, back-drop of expansive panorama of the south	Easy	½	295843	Y
45	Cronk ny Arrey Laa	Short hill walk with awesome coastal cliff views to Calf of Man	Easy	¾	232747	
46	Eary Cushlin and Lag ny Keeilley	Grassland and clifftop walk in remote and peaceful spot, ancient chapel	Easy to steep	½-2½	225762	
47	South Barrule	Hill walk with sweeping views of whole Island, very significant pre-historic site	Moderate	1½	258759	
48	Foxdale Mines	Historic industrial buildings in rugged, bleak upland setting	Easy	1	295843	
49	Niarbyl Bay	Picturesque bay and clifftop walk, chance to straddle two continents	Easy	1	212777	
50	Glen Maye	Walk through profusely vegetated glen to beach, dramatic waterfall	Easy to moderate	1	236798	
51	Garey Ny Cloie, St John's	The most varied woodland on the entire Island – Global Tree Trail	Easy	¾	280812	Y
52	Tynwald Hill & Cooill y Ree Gardens	Place of national significance, re-creation of Manx woodlands through time	Easy	½	278820	Y
53	National Park and Arboretum	Extensive park and woodland in beautiful setting	Easy to moderate	½-1½	279818	Y
54	The Raggat	Woodland and riverside walk, where loved ones are remembered	Easy	½	242829	Y
55	Peel Hill and Corrin's Tower	Hill walk with impressive views of Peel's Castle and harbour, 19th century folly	Easy to moderate	1½	246682	
56	Peel Headland	Glorious views of Peel Castle and surrounding countryside, a look back into the town's interesting past	Easy	1¼	250842	
57	Glen Helen	Walk through varied and scenic woodland by river running through deep gorge, waterfall	Easy	1½	295843	
58	Spooyt Vane Waterfall and Keeill	Woodland walk, impressive waterfall and remains of ancient chapel	Easy	½	308888	
59	Glen Wyllin	Woodland walk and Nature Reserve, dramatic river cliffs, rounded off with a stroll to the coast	Easy	1½	313903	
60	Bishopscourt Glen	Woodland and river walk, with cave, two ponds and a model of Tynwald Hill	Easy	1	329925	Y
61	Glen Dhoo	Remote countryside walk, utterly tranquil, historic farm buildings	Easy	1	352919	
62	Close Sartfield	Lush flower meadows, curraghs show how Island may have looked 15,000 years ago	Easy	½-1	358956	Y
63	Ballaugh Old Church and The Cronk	Delightful hamlet with truly historic church, countryside walk to a quiet beach	Easy	¾	340958	Y

CONTENTS

INTRODUCTION

A treasure chest of gems

For such a small island, the Isle of Man has a wealth of interesting, scenic and often unusual places and sites to explore. There are many well-known places whose signifigance and history are well described in tourist guides. And if you have not already visited places such as Laxey Wheel, Peel Castle and Castle Rushen you really should do so.

However, there are a multitude of equally interesting, curious and fascinating places which are either not so well-known or stories about them are not so familiar. Many people, even those who have lived for a long time on the Island, may not know that they are there or have come across their interesting tales. So if you are interested in finding the answer to these questions . . .

- Where can you stand with your feet in different continents?
- Where can you see a monument as old as Stonehenge?
- Where can you stand atop a tower in the shape of a lock?
- Where can you stand next to a wizard?
- Where can you sit in a cave where a Bishop hid himself?
- Where can you see 7 Kingdoms at the same time?
- Where is Sir Norman Wisdom's grave?
- Where is the real Fairy Bridge?

. . . this book is for you. If you want to explore the Island and discover its hidden gems this guide lists over 60 of them. If you want to find out fascinating snippets of information about slightly more familiar places this guide should help. Each section has a brief description of the walk and what you will see, together with interesting anecdotes and stories.

Easy walks for non-walkers

These places of interest have been chosen because they can be accessed by a relatively short and easy walk – two miles or less. You do not need to be a walker or a hiker as the routes are easy to follow and most just require a good pair of shoes on your feet. In particular these walks would appeal to those . . .

- Who fancy going for a brief walk and want to try somewhere different and have a purpose to their stroll
- Who want to go out somewhere for an hour or so when the evenings are lighter longer in spring and summer
- With children who would like to go for a brief walk, rather than hike, and find something that will arouse their curiosity along the way
- Who are visiting for a holiday, or to watch the bike races, and want to spend a few hours seeing sights that visitors would not normally see.

This book acts a personal tour guide as you walk along, drawing your attention to interesting snippets of history, geography and culture along the route.

Most walks are short and gentle, on the flat or mild gradients only. Indeed many might suit those whose mobility may be restricted as the terrain is flat or only gently ascending and the walking surface is even and in good condition. If there is a flight of steps they are usually short. Occasionally there may be a kissing gate or stile to negotiate – these will be mentioned in the description. Such walks are indicated in the Tables of Walks.

7

There are a few walks that require slightly more effort, and proper walking footwear is advised, although they are easy to navigate. The additional effort required to walk to summits such as Snaefell, South Barrule and Cronk ny Arrey Laa is more than repaid by the awesome, breath-taking views that you will experience, and which photographs struggle to do justice to.

Do repeat the walks at different times of the year. Spring is invariably the best time to catch wildflowers and summer is when plants, bushes and grass grow in abundance and can really change the appearance of the land. Autumn is the season when nature has a different palette of colours.

Practical information before you set off

All these walks can be done without the need for a map. However, I would suggest referring to the OS Landranger Map Sheet 95 (scale 1:50,000 or 1.25 inches to the mile). This will not only help you find the start point for each stroll but will help you appreciate better the landscape, monuments and settlements that you may see on your trip.

The start of all walks can be accessed by car or motorbike and they finish where you started so there is no need to cover extra miles to return to your vehicle. For those without their own transport bus and rail services take you to, or close to, many of the start points. Bus and rail routes and times are available at www.iombusandrail.info , on (01624) 662525 or a printed timetable is available from the Visitor Centre in the Sea Terminal (Douglas) or other visitor sites.

Checking the weather in advance is advised for any walk – there can be few people who enjoy walking in the rain if it can be avoided, even if your journey is a short one. Certain walks are well above sea level and having no low cloud and good visibility really adds to the experience. All the Island radio stations and news websites carry weather forecasts for one to two days ahead. I find the most detailed is on http://www.bbc.co.uk/weather/3042237 which gives hour-by-hour forecasts for next day.

The Port e Vullen walk involves crossing a beach for which you will need a low tide. To check tide times I use http://www.thebeachguide.co.uk hit the button for Isle of Man, select a beach location from the map and click on weather and tides button.

Agneash

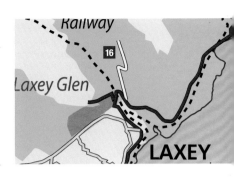

Description: tranquil upland valley looking towards Snaefell, historic mining site; easy to moderate 2 miles (can be extended to 4)

OS map reference: 431861

Take A2 to Laxey, take turning towards Laxey Wheel, and continue onwards for a mile. There is some parking in Agneash village, otherwise park in Laxey and walk up the road.

On the left fork of the road in Agneash there is a Greenway sign just by a gate leading on to the village green. Follow the road, this is the route that miners would have taken from Laxey village everyday over 150 years ago: although a small number would have lived in Agneash itself. Situated at the top of Laxey Valley at an altitude of one thousand feet, Snaefell mine was the highest major mine on the Island. Mining began in about 1856 and lead and zinc were the principal minerals extracted. The final depth of the mine was over one thousand feet. It closed in 1908, although, as we will see, 1897 is a far more significant date.

Immediately there are views ahead of Snaefell and, on the left, of the Mountain Railway. The railway from Laxey to the summit was built in a few months and opened in August 1895: all the passenger cars date from that year. Continue through the gate, the road gives way to a gravel track. Blackcurrant bushes line the path – this would be an excellent walk in early autumn. As you pass through another gate the ascent briefly becomes moderate rather than easy. You are now in open countryside with the steeply sloping Laxey Valley on either side. You should be able to make out that it is a U-shape which has been gouged by extremely thick glaciers moving down from Snaefell tens of thousands of years ago. At the bottom of the U the valley is a narrow V-shape which has been incised by the river whose source is near the Verandah on the Mountain Road.

On the right is a small derelict farm (these are known in Manx as *tholtans*) which has been overtaken by vegetation. The walls are locally sourced grey slate streaked brown and red from the mineral deposits. The land around here would not have provided much of a living so the farmer may have supplemented his income by working in the mine. The path slopes gradually downhill passing another gate. The railway is closer now and you may here the rattle of the carriage.

On the right there is a ribbon waterfall. Cross over a bridge. On the left is a quite a substantial two storey, ruined dwelling with only the end wall and chiollagh (fireplace) still remaining. This may be where senior officials connected with the mine lived. The path climbs gradually and the sound of the Laxey River tumbling down the valley becomes apparent. Pass through a gate with another derelict building on the left

9

– curiously the doorway is on the opposite side of the building to the track. If you intend to walk just two miles this would be an appropriate place to turn around.

The immense sloping barren spoil heaps now come into view. These comprise the mined rocks which were crushed in order to extract the prized minerals. The waste heaps were known as 'deads' as they contained traces of lead which made it a struggle for plants to live on them. On the right is the Mine Captain's house which has a pair of gateposts which seem to be better preserved than the building itself. Its walls were rendered, rather than left as bare stone, which would have made this structure an impressive sight.

At the foot of the deads there is a mine building dating to the 19th century, however, most of the other ones date from the 1950s when a company was reworking the spoil heaps to extract more minerals. This area of wasteland and derelict buildings has been promoted by the Government as a film location – from certain angles it does have a post-apocalyptic feel. Inside one of these buildings on the right hand wall there is a plaque commemorating four off-road bikers who died in the previous decade. Beyond this building a narrow path leads to a chimney from where one can see ribbon waterfalls.

On a low platform to the right of the site is a tablet with the names of the twenty miners who lost their lives in a tragic accident in 1897. On Monday, 10th May the morning shift of thirty five men descended into the shaft. Shortly afterwards, several men came to the surface in an exhausted condition stating that the mine was full of foul gas. Rescuers started a descent of the shaft to assess the situation. They met several men trying to make their way up the ladder out of the mine and fighting for breath. Between 250 and 350 feet below the surface men were found still alive but unconscious. The rescue continued until late afternoon when the last of 15 survivors was brought to the surface. Twenty men who were deeper in the mine died. A fire deep underground had reduced the oxygen levels and increased carbon monoxide levels sufficient to overcome a man in 7 minutes. Only three days earlier H M Inspector of Mines had reported that *'the ventilation was very good'*.

Most of the surnames are clearly Manx but two, Senocles and Kelly, are more commonly associated with Cornwall. Tin mining had been long established in this county and miners from there were much respected and sought after across the British Isles and further afield.

Return along the same route that you arrived by.

Arragon House

Description: woodland and stream walk around grounds of a mansion, riot of colour in spring, an ostentation of peacocks: easy, ½ mile
OS map reference: 316705
Take the Old Castletown Road (A25) from Douglas and turn left down a minor road (B25) signed Port Grenaugh. There is parking at the end just before the beach.

Follow the public footpath sign through a black, tipped with gold, kissing gate. The path skirts round the estate and is immaculately well kept. At first it follows a meandering brook uphill which is flanked by interesting plants and bushes including a few stands of bamboo. There are ornate bridges that look oriental in design. On the right is a meadow which is home to vast multitude of daffodils.

Walk through another kissing gate and the path turns left opening up the beautiful vista of a tree-lined alley with spring bulbs in profusion. Over the wall on the left one can see the well-kept gardens of Arragon House, and on the right the fields are home to geese and donkeys. The front of the house itself is revealed on the far side of another kissing gate and, if lucky, you will encounter several peacocks, including a few white ones.

Previously the house was known as Seafield House and was a hotel for many decades in the 20th century. In the 1980s it reverted to a private house: and to the name Arragon which was derived from the historic name of the estate (*Ard Roagan* or *Roagan's Height*) in which it was built.

Downhill past the house the bridge crosses over a delightful pond and water garden. Retrace one's steps to return to the start.

For those interested in the Iron Age, Cronk ny Merriu, the remains of promontory fort, is nearby Port Grenaugh. Facing the beach follow a path on the left marked with a blue Coastal Footpath sign. You will reach the site in a few minutes. The fort dates back almost 2,000 years, with the bank and ditch creating a defensive homestead. Later, a rectangular building from the Norse period stood here which was part of a system of coastal lookout posts. Cronk ny Merriu is a Celtic name meaning 'Hill of death' – the Celts migrated to the Isle of Man several hundred years before the Vikings arrived.

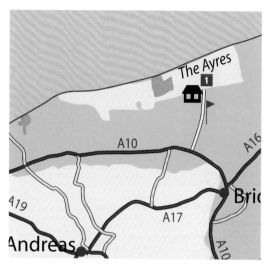

Ayres Nature Reserve

Description: low-lying heathland and sand dune coastline, paradise for birdwatchers, Area of Special Scientific Interest: easy, ½-2 miles.
OS map reference: 438038
Proceed north of Ramsey on the A10 through Bride. The minor road to the Reserve is on the right one mile after Bride. There is a car park at the end by the Visitor Centre (open 2-5pm from May to mid-September).

The Ayres is a site of major ecological significance, parts having been designated as an Area of Special Scientific Interest and as a National Nature Reserve. The main feature is the large area of lichen heath, grey in colour – a habitat which only occurs in small patches in the UK. Lichen thrives in environments with extremely low pollution levels, so it loves it here. Dozens of different bird species that are spotted here are recorded on a whiteboard outside the Visitor Centre. There are breeding colonies of arctic and little terns and cormorants, oystercatchers, curlews, lapwings, mallard and shelduck are often seen. Inside the Visitor Centre has a display about the ecology, geology and history of the Ayres.

The first place to head for is the elevated viewing platform which gives 360 degree views for miles around. To the right of this is a wooden walkway into the dunes which one can use to reach the shoreline. Heading north, to your right as you look out to sea, is the start of one of the designated trails marked by the occasional red post. This one starts across the dune tops and after a few hundred yards heads inland to the heath. As you walk from the beach inland you can see how sand can turn to land on which turf grows turf with a heath eventually establishing itself. The soil gets progressively darker and richer as more organic material cumulates.

There are three marked Nature Trails of different lengths which wind through the marram dunes and onto the expanse of heath inland. They are marked by red, blue and black coloured posts – leaflet available in Visitor Centre. Alternatively, walk along the shore where oystercatchers and seals are often to be found.

Further along the A10 there are minor roads leading to other heath and dune locations such as Blue Point and Rue Point.

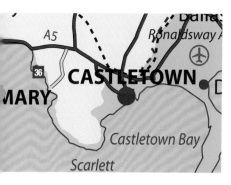

Balladoole, Castletown

Description: impressive Viking burial on site with expansive coastal and inland views, lake in disued quarry: easy, ½ mile
OS map reference: 246682
Leave Castletown on the A5 towards Port St Mary. After the by-pass take the first left down a minor road, signposted Pooil Vaaish Quarry. Just before the bend in the road park up off the road: there is a sign on the right for the path to Balladoole.

Proceed through the gate and take the path on the left which winds gently uphill to a small plateau – there are wonderful views to south of Gansey Bay, Port St Mary and Chicken Rock (off the Calf of Man) and northwards to South Barrule and the chain of hills in the centre of the island to Snaefell. The views afforded by this site were significant reason why it was chosen originally as an Iron Age hillfort in first few centuries AD. The rampart that encircles the site is at least 6 feet higher than the area outside and it is likely that it was considerably higher when it was built – but the stone has been purloined by farmers to build walls. To

be able to command a view over many miles of surrounding land was an important defensive asset.

Immediately on your left is an oval of stones stretching over 40 feet which mark the site where a Viking boat burial, dating back to between 850AD and 950AD, was discovered in 1945. The team that excavated the site was led by the famous archaeologist Gerhard Bersu, a German national who was held in one of the many internment camps that were established on the Isle of Man during World War 2. The boat contained the bodies of a Viking nobleman and a woman, who it is believed was his servant and was sacrificed and buried with him. Also buried were many everyday items such as clothes, tools, food and drink: the remains of a horse and a shield were found but no sword or other weapon. These were all buried alongside the warrior as Vikings thought that they would be needed in the afterlife. Interestingly, the long ship was buried over earlier Christian graves. These graves contained several people. One woman whose remains were excavated and sent for DNA analysis was found to be from North Africa. One can only wonder at her journey from there to the Isle of Man.

The outline stones of a small chapel (*Keeill Vael*) dating between 900AD and 1000AD is at the far side of the site. Further round on the left is a Bronze Age grave dating to 1000 BC. It was common in this period for bodies to be buried in stone boxes (cists), measuring about 3 feet by 2 feet, in the ground. Bodies were often preserved (mummified) by keeping them in peat for a year before burial and put into the cist in a crouch or foetal position.

The south west corner of the site overlooks a steep-sided former limestone quarry which has now filled with fresh water and provides a safe haven for birds.

Ballafayle

Description: grassland walk to monuments both ancient and modern, stunning coastal views: easy ½ mile
OS Map Reference: 478901
Take the A2 north past Laxey and at The Hibernian turn left on to the A15. Proceed for a mile and take a left turn (at same junction there is a right turn) up a narrow road flanked by hedges. At the top of the hill there are spaces to park off the road.

Ballafayle was deliberately chosen as a ceremonial burial site as it has commanding views to the north and east and it can be seen from a distance. The site would have acted as a very visible statement of the ancient inhabitants' importance and stature in the area. It is very close to another site, Cashtal yn Ard, so there might have been a bit of one-

upmanship going on between the two communities! The cairn was excavated in 1926 and the remains were dated to the Neolithic period, 2000-1500 BC. The most prominent feature is a wedge shaped cairn containing many stones fused by heat, suggesting that cremations took place. There is one more prominent standing stone by a paved forecourt which would possibly have been at the entrance to the burial chambers.

The site has several other treasures. If you go through the wooden gate immediately to the left is a stone on which there is an extract from the Island's most famous poet TE Brown who lived in the 19th century. On the right is an almost circular stone wall, it looks like it is modelled on an upland sheep shelter, which has a bench where you can take in the views towards Maughold. In spring and summer the fields are populated by sheep.

In front are two modern sculptures of ravens, a bird that is strongly associated with Norse mythology and which adorns the Isle of Man coat of arms. Beyond this is a tablet commemorating Sir Charles Kerruish which shows the direction of different parts of Britain across the Irish Sea. Sir Charles was perhaps the most well-known Manx politician. He was the Speaker of the House of Keys from 1962 to 1990, making him the longest serving Speaker in any Parliament in the Commonwealth.

Return to the road and cross it to view the Rullic ny Qakerny which is the site of an ancient keeill (ancient chapels, often built over a thousand years ago) given over as a burial ground for Quakers. The white stone is quartzite which was used to indicate the location of keeills as it could catch the light and be seen from a distance. As the headstone says, Manx Quakers suffered persecution and imprisonment for the faith and in 1665 they were banished from the Isle of Man. Many settled in America and one relation of these has an interesting story to tell. Betsy Ross was born in 1752 of a Manx Quaker family. She was a seamstress who lived in Philadelphia and the story has it that she made the first Stars and Stripes in 1777, as she was a friend of George Washington.

Ballaglass Glen

Description: idyllic glen walk following the spectacular Cornaa river, numerous waterfalls: mainly easy, 1-1½ miles.

OS map reference: 468898

Take the A2 coast road from Laxey to Ramsey. At Hibernian turn right on to A15. After a mile turn right down a minor road which soon crosses Manx Electric Railway (MER) track. There is a car park by the entrance to the glen.

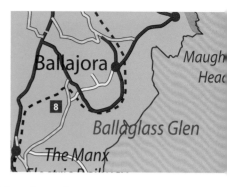

The glen was acquired by the Forestry Board in 1952 from its previous owner The Manx Electric Railway Company who had been developing it to encourage visits by MER passengers. The name Ballaglass translates as *'Farm of the stream'*.

Cross the wide footbridge and go through the gate on your left along a well-made gravel path which follows the river downstream. Immediately on the left by a waterfall is the remains of a mine building – you can see a cog wheel on the outside wall, this was used to provide water to wash the lead ore. The Great Mona Mining Company which extracted lead, zinc and copper operated here in the 1850s and 1860s. There are several small waterfalls and plunge pools as the river quickly finds its way downhill. The woodland has thousands of bluebells which bloom in the spring. The trees and plants in this glen are typical of the sort that would have covered much of the higher land 8,000 years ago when man first started to live on the Isle of Man.

The path diverts away from the river to reach a cottage, behind which is a delightful wizard carved from a tree trunk. A rocky path bears left past the cottage, through an iron gate to the riverbank. By the gate is another path with a wooden railing on the

left. Pause at the bench to admire how, for such a small river, the Cornaa has cut very deeply into the slate rocks. Leaving the bench there is a path off to your left going slightly uphill which takes you back to the cottage. Just at the corner of the building there is a track off to your left going gently uphill through the shade of the woods.

For the full walk through the glen continue straight on ignoring the left and right turns and you will come close to the MER track. As the main path levels off, by a wide tree trunk there is a small path off to the left with a wooden handrail and steps down to the river. Here one has a close up view of the strength of the river as it tumbles over the rocks. Bear right down the riverside path following the handrail: it climbs gently uphill past further waterfalls. On the left is a derelict white two-storey building: this is a corn mill last used in 1951. Continue past this on the path that follows the river, there is a wooden walkway taking you over muddy ground. Don't take the bridge that crosses the river; instead follow a narrow path beside the river. The path effectively stops by an archway which is a bridge carrying the MER.

Turn round to retrace your steps but this time use the bridge to cross the river, so that now it is on your left. Over a wooden walkway there are a couple of steps that take your round a tree in the middle of the path. When in full spate the sound of the river can become quiet deafening. Here you may see a group of adventurous people in wetsuits and helmets who are scrambling up the rocky course of the river or jumping off the rocks into the plunge pools below. The path descends by steps and crosses a bridge. Turn right and continue uphill using the handrail.

At the top of that path cross straight over the main track heading along a narrower path through the woods. This passes a curiously low bench which appears to be made out of wooden pallets. Join a wider track and turn right and you will now see the car park in front of you.

Ballaugh Old Church and The Cronk

Description: delightful hamlet with truly historic church, countryside walk to a quiet beach: easy, ¾ mile.
OS map reference: 340958
Take the A3 to Ballaugh and turn left (A10) through the village: follow the road for just over a mile until you reach the old church. Follow the road left round the church and after the right bend there is parking off the road.

Walk back to the church and before entering admire the twin gate pillars which, legend has it, were purposefully built leaning together. Another legend claims that if they ever touch it will be the end of the world! The Old Church of Saint Mary's de Ballaugh is mentioned in a Papal Bull of 1231 and the earliest recorded Rector dates from 1408. The cupola, which was built in 1717 when the church was extended, houses the bell which is rung from the outside – a relatively uncommon feature. Inside it is very simple with a tiny vestry and an 11th century stone cross immediately on the right. The churchyard has several very old and worn gravestones.

Return towards where you parked and take the narrow road signed Ballaugh Shore. The road winds down to the shore where there is a car park. There are views for several miles south towards Peel Hill and north as far as Jurby. The low cliffs are made from blown sand, which was deposited by retreating glaciers about 15,000 years ago, and are easily eroded: concrete and granite blocks have been placed up and down the coastline in an attempt to halt this. Unfortunately, this just tends to shift the problem of erosion along to undefended stretches of the coastline.

If you walk round the rocks to the left you can briefly follow the river upstream before the vegetation becomes too dense and halts one's progress. Further up this river there used to be a small inland harbour, which could accommodate a dozen fishing boats, that has since silted up. Historians point out that Ballaugh may be a shortened version of *Balla ny Loghey* which translates as 'settlement of the lake' – referring to historic times when this place, close to Ballaugh Curraghs, was far more marshy and populated by pools of water than it is now.

Return back along the road to the hamlet.

Ballure Reservoir and Glen

Description: woodland walk down to and round to a delightful little reservoir: easy, ½ mile. Option of walk down glen to the beach: easy to moderate, ¾ mile.
OS map reference: 453930
Follow the TT Course (A18) from Ramsey climbing past the Hairpin. As the road straightens past the Waterworks there is a car park on the left before you reach the Gooseneck.

Go through the metal gate at the end of the car park. Pass the pale blue picnic benches, the wide track goes through trees. It curves right and levels off giving you views of North Barrule, the second highest summit on the Island. The path continues downhill past some more characteristically coloured benches. Proceed through a wooden gate past an information board for the reservoir. After another wooden gate turn right: at the green footpath sign follow the path left downhill. Through the gate to the edge of the reservoir. It was opened in 1884 and is approximately 35 foot deep with a capacity of 15 million gallons. The reservoir is nowadays used only recreationally and not for water supply.

An information board outlines several walks in the area. A suggestion is to proceed anti-clockwise on the perimeter path which you find by going through the gate to the immediate right of the board. There is a well-made gravel path with occasional steps to take one over the streams that flow into the reservoir. Steps lead down to the water's edge to accommodate anglers. A significant flight of steps take you up into the woodland with great views down to the water. The path levels off into a constant corridor of bluebells if you are here in the spring. In

between the occasional roar of bikes as they climb the TT Course, you may catch adorable bird song. The path drops down a few steps and turns left through a gate towards the reservoir dam wall.

You can retrace your steps to the car park, remembering to turn left up through the small wooden gate, rather than going through the blue gate. Or alternatively one can extend the walk through the glen.

To extend the walk had back towards the zig-zag path and just before you reach it going downhill there is a blue 6 bar metal gate. Immediately take the right fork. The glen was created by the Ramsey Water Company after their waterworks was opened in 1885. It was privately owned for several decades until it was sold to the Forestry Board in 1959.

The path slopes gently downhill through the trees – unfortunately these prevent one from having a clear view of the river on the right. Where the path levels there are delightful glades to the left which are carpeted with bluebells in the spring. The path is lined with wild garlic in places: this plant has contributed to the town's name, as the Manx for Ramsey is *Rhumsaa* which translates as 'wild garlic river'. After the path hairpins right it emerges on to the Ramsey road. Turn left to cross the Manx Electric Railway track and immediately cross the road and take a narrow path on the right where there is a gap in the wall.

Owing to its closeness to the sea and the fact that the glen used to be quite overgrown it has a connection with smuggling. The notorious *Carras-dhoo* men would use it to bring contraband ashore and hide it until it could be distributed to the nearby towns and villages.

Follow the path, there are some short flights of concrete steps, to reach the river. The slightly uneven track follows the river which soon goes through a charming archway and reaches the sea. From here the *Carras-dhoo* men would light fires to trick ships and lead them to run aground on the shore. This stretch of bay is where Prince Albert, Queen Victoria's husband, was rowed ashore during an impromptu royal visit in 1847. Prince Albert's party made its way up the glen to eventually reach the hill overlooking Ramsey on which the Albert Tower was constructed.

Retrace your steps to the main road and to bottom of the footpath that you have used. You can either return by the same route or take the narrow tarmac road (public footpath sign for The Gooseneck). If you follow the road on the left you can see the deep gorge carved by the river. You soon come to the dam wall of the reservoir, just before this on the left is evidence of an earlier small pond which is now overgrown with plants. This was one of two smaller reservoirs which were replaced by the main one – they were unable to cope with the increasing demand as Ramsey grew rapidly due to tourism in the late 19th century.

Take the path on the right up towards the information board and return to the car park by the way you arrived.

Beinn y Phott

Description: relatively easy short walk to summit with panoramic views stretching over a dozen miles: easy, ¾ mile.
OS map reference: 389859
Park the car in a lay-by, just beyond the cattle grid, a few yards down the B10 from its junction with the Mountain Road (A18) – very close to the Marshal's hut at Brandywell.

This is a gem of a hill. The going is easy over grassland, unless it has rained heavily recently you should not get wet feet. At 1791 feet, it is only a couple of hundred feet off the height of the highest peak Snaefell and it affords very similar views. Yet it is not cluttered by tram rails, radio masts, concrete paths and buildings. Nor by people. The name Beinn y Phott (known locally as 'penny pot') comes from the Manx *Beinn y Foaid* which translates loosely as 'Turf Mountain' – the slopes were a good source of peat in times gone by.

The summit is visible from the car parking spot. Cross the road and walk round to the right of the wooden railing. For the first 50 yards head slightly to the left of the exact direction of the peak in order to pick up the trail. There is a relatively well-worn route all the way to the top. Half way along on the left there is a large white boulder on its own which must have been left by the retreating glaciers at the end of the last Ice Age about 15,000 years ago.

The summit is marked by a low cairn with a small collection of rocks which looks like it once acted as a sheep shelter. You have just climbed, what is known in hill-bagging circles as, a Dewey which is a term used to denote a hill in England or Wales over 500 metres (1,640 feet) in elevation, but below 2,000 feet (609.6 metres). A hill above 2,000 feet in classified as a mountain.

From here one can see a dozen or so of hill summits in the north and centre of the Island as well as views of Douglas to the east. The topography of the surrounding hills is particularly efficient at funnelling the sound of the motorbikes as they enjoy the unrestricted speeds of the Mountain Road several hundred feet below.

Descend by exactly the same route as you came – heading towards your vehicle which is just a smudge in the distance.

Bishopscourt Glen

Description: woodland and river walk, with cave, two
ponds and a model of Tynwald Hill: easy, 1 mile.
OS map reference: 329925
Follow the A3 (TT Course) out of Kirk Michael, just after
Rhencullen there is Bishops Court on the left, opposite
there is a lay-by.

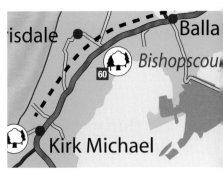

The entrance to Bishopscourt Glen is through a black
wooden gate between two white gateposts. Bishops
Court, across the road, was formerly the residence of the Bishop of
Sodor and Man. In the late 17th and early 18th centuries Bishop Wilson
arranged the planting of several thousand trees to form the glen as his
private garden. It was owned privately until it was bought by the
Forestry Board in 1963.

There is an information board by the entrance. The glen has a path
which circles the woodland, begin your circuit by taking the path on the
left. After a few yards across the river is the stepped mound of Mount
Aeolus which we will explore on the way back. The walk has a profusion
of spring bulbs and wild garlic flowers. Keep the river on your right,
ignoring the small footbridge, as the path climbs gradually. You may
hear it before you see it, but you will encounter a mill pond with a large
flock of ducks. Keep on the low level path, not taking the one on the
left that rises slightly. On the right there is a small stone bridge where
you may want to dangle your feet in the waterfall.

The next section could be called 'Rhododendron Alley'. Cross over the
river at two places so it is now on your left, still take the lower level path
that follows closer to the river. Cross a stone bridge, the path slopes
gradually uphill: proceed straight on when a track intersects across. On the
left, carved into a precariously hanging tree trunk, is a small seat. By a
wooden retaining wall to the right is a small path up to a cave. Known as
the 'Cave of the Winds', it is where Bishop George Murray allegedly took
refuge from angry locals at the time of the Potato Tithe Riots in 1825 –
they were refusing to pay the tax on their staple food to the church.

Return to the path climbing uphill, cross a narrow stone bridge so
the river on is on your left. After short flight of steps the path is now
bending back on the return loop. Cross the wooden bridge the path
bearing right, walk through a delightful archway made by a curved tree
trunk. Path descends steeply to cross the river and temporarily re-join
the original way. Bear left where there is a row of tree trunks cut into
little seats. Cross the slate bridge and at the next stone bridge bear left
following a cinder track. Pass a small pond on the right and you will
come across the larger pond again.

Path forks left down a couple of steps to a wooden bridge, follow
the path as it curves left and you will see Mount Aeolus. This was built

as a replica of Tynwald Hill in St Johns, where an open air parliament is held annually on Tynwald Day (the Isle of Man's National Day in early July). There is a stone sign saying that the mound was built to commemorate the victory of an English fleet against the French off the coast of the Island in 1760. *'The Aeolus'* was the name of the Royal Naval Ship which was captained by John Eliot and which lead the attack.

Head back to the gate to conclude the walk.

The Braaid

Description: well preserved Iron Age and Viking homesteads in open countryside: easy, ½ mile.
OS map reference: 325765
The Braaid is midway between Douglas and Foxdale on A24. One can park in a lay-by across the road and that is close to the path that leads to The Braaid, or there is car park a hundred yards further on.

Follow the path through a gate on the north side of the road, proceed through two stiles and as the path bears left you will have a full view of the site. There are information boards which tell the story of the site and give an impression of what the buildings may have looked like.

The Braaid was first occupied in either the Neolithic and Bronze age periods. These original settlers built a stone roundhouse which has been dated to 600AD. Later the site was used by the Vikings as a farmstead and the two longhouses are dated around 900AD. They are the best preserved structures of this period on the Island and clearly show the different ingrained approaches to house building of the two peoples. It is said that the shape of the longhouse mimics that of Viking longboats, although it is unsure if this is deliberate or coincidental. This is the only place on the Island that indicates the continuity between the early Celtic inhabitants and the later Viking invaders – although there may have been continuity it is debateable if there was much harmony!

The Viking longhouses are nearest to you. Their walls are very thick (over a yard) to enable them to bear the weight of the roof. The houses are unusually long for a Viking farmstead. The second longhouse is slightly smaller and it is though that it was used to house livestock in the winter. On the far side, the Celtic round house is also relatively large example of its kind. This might be an indication of the size of the family groups or that building materials were in abundance nearby.

The site has excellent views of the surrounding countryside and the hills stretching northwards on the island. This is likely to have been a factor in choosing the site originally as it gives early warning of anyone approaching.

Bradda Glen

Description: clifftop path round bay of Victorian resort: easy, ½ mile
OS Map reference: 195697
Take the main road (A32) through Port Erin and round the top of the bay. Continue straight on up the hill past the apartment buildings and park near the entrance of Bradda Glen.

Proceed through the Bradda Glen arch, made from local slate, following the sloping path past bluebells and wild garlic in the spring. After a minute take a sharp left turn. There are steps down to the beach but we continue straight on along the main path round the bay. There are a few steps down and up, then the path rises up to a metal footbridge. There is a great view back to Bradda Head and Milner's Tower. This was built in 1871 as a viewing tower in memory of William Milner of the then-famous Milner's Safe Co. Ltd., maker of fire-resistant safes and a local philanthropist, who built a breakwater to shelter fishing boats in Port Erin bay. His tower is built in the shape of a key.

As the path curves round you see the remains of an open-air salt water swimming pool. It was called Traie Meanagh which is Middle Bay in Manx. The pool was thriving in the period before the Frist World War and allowed mixed bathing – very progressive for that period! As late as the 1960s galas were held every Wednesday with short speed swimming events and fun events like egg and spoon and balloon races. There were bathing beauty competitions and the Squadron Cup was presented to the winner of the weekly swimming and games competition that was contested by teams from different hotels. The pool closed to bathers in 1981, and was a fish farm until the early 1990s, since when it has been derelict.

As the path rises take the right fork to continue along the headland: glorious views of the sandy expanse of Port Erin beach open up. Port Erin was a grand and popular holiday resort in the late 19th and early 20th centuries when visitor numbers were at their peak. It was, and still is, the terminus of the steam railway from Douglas. Continue the walk by following the green railing, there are plenty of benches to sit on to take in the view. Finally, a flight of steps takes one up to the main road by the Port Erin Royal Hotel.

To return to the start either turn left on the road or retrace your way round the path for a different series of views to the outward journey.

Bradda Head and Milner's Tower

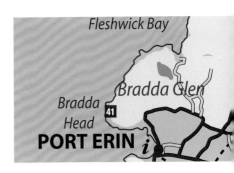

Description: glen walk with climb over open grassland to famous landmark with spectacular sea cliff views: easy to moderate, 1½ miles.
OS Map reference: 195697
Take the main road through Port Erin (A32) and round the top of the bay. Continue straight on up the hill past the apartment buildings and park near the entrance of Bradda Glen.

Take the tarmac path through the Bradda Glen entrance archway which descends through greenery heavy with the scent of wild garlic in spring. Pass the tearooms and pause a moment. In the mid nineteenth century the owner of the Bellevue Zoo in Manchester built a holiday home on this ground which was later converted into a holiday camp using wooden huts that had been used at the Knockaloe internment camp during World War 1.

Follow the footpath signed Coronation Path. Keep the low wall on your left as you head towards the open grassed area. The main route towards Corrin's Tower undulates and is briefly steep in a couple of places: use a raised wooden platform on the left heading over the rocky ground. Alternatively for a gentler climb, as the path levels take a track on the right across the open grassland and head towards the tower. The name Bradda Head derives from the old English word 'Bradhou' meaning broad headland.

There are excellent views south towards the Sound and the Calf and Man from the top of the tower which can be accessed by an internal spiral staircase. This was built in 1871 as a tribute to William Milner of the then-famous Milner's Safe Co. Ltd., maker of fire-resistant safes in Liverpool. In the later part of his life he lived in Port Erin and was a great benefactor to the town. The funds were raised by public donations and the design of the tower is said to represent the shape of the key to his very first safe. The tower was meant to be built in secret (how that could be achieved when it is in such a prominent position?). However, when Milner found out he donated much of the building cost himself.

The Mourne Mountains of Ireland can sometimes be seen from the summit. In 1931 "Kodak's World's Best Photograph" was taken from here (plaque on tower).

Return by the way that you came.

Bride and Point of Ayre

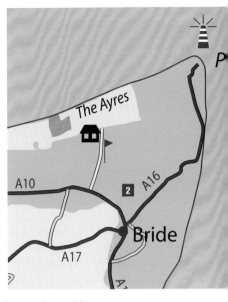

Description: Bride – churchyard with Sir Norman Wisdom's grave; Point of Ayre – expansive beach and lighthouses on tip of the Island: easy, ½ mile
OS map reference: Bride 449012; Point of Ayre 468048
Bride village is on A10 north of Ramsey. There is a car park opposite the church.

As you walk from the car park note the wall of the public toilets which has been decorated by a series of delightful mosaics created by local schoolchildren to mark the Millennium in 2000.

The church in Bride has a long history. In 1188 it was a Rectory held by the Abbot of the Cistercian monastery in Furness, Lancashire and the church was built on the site of an even earlier keeill. The keeill, whose foundations are in the adjacent churchyard, was a very small chapel dating from 7th century that was used as a place of worship by itinerant monks. The keeill was only designed for solitary worship and the monk would say prayers to the local people who gathered outside. The current church was rebuilt between 1869-76 – although it has a record of all its vicars dating back to 1377.

Over the main door is the sundial from the 19th century which was the only means of telling the time until the clock was donated in the 1960s.

Inside the church on the left is a stained glass window depicting St Bridget after whom the church is dedicated, and the village itself is named. St Bridget was one of the early Christian missionaries who came over to the Isle of Man: she is always depicted holding a flame. The collection of crosses from the Norse period and are about 1,000 years old.

On leaving the church follow the road round to the right where you can enter the churchyard through the gate. If you follow the main path to the end on the right is the grave of the famous comic actor Sir Norman Wisdom which is adorned by his trademark flat cap. Norman was a cultural icon on the Island, as well as being a cult in Albania, where he was refer to as 'Mr Pitkin' after the character that he played in films. He lived in Andreas for many years where he named his house Ballalough – Gaelic for *'House of Laughs'*. His statue sits on a bench outside the Sefton Hotel on Douglas Promenade – in which a bar is themed around him.

Return to your vehicle for the second part of this visit. Turn right out of the car park and follow the sign for Point of Ayre which is about 3 miles away. Just before the lighthouse turn right, signed The Shore, where there is plenty of parking.

Ayre comes from the Norse word *Eyrr* meaning gravel bank. At the tip of the Island strong currents run immediately offshore which leads to the shingle shifting shape with every tide. The coastline here is actually extending out into the sea which contrasts with the sandy cliff coastline stretching either side of it which is retreating due to erosion.

The main lighthouse is the oldest on the Isle of Man and was first lit in 1818. It was built by Robert Stevenson, the grandfather of the famous author Robert Louis Stevenson. The light has a nominal range of around 19 miles and can be seen clearly from across the water in Galloway, south-west Scotland. Owing to the continuous accumulation of shingle and gravel deposited by the strong currents, a smaller light commonly referred to as 'Winkie' had to be built to the seaward side of the main tower in 1899 and re-positioned in 1950. In 2005, the fog horn was de-commissioned.

You are very likely to see at least one of the many ferries that cross between Stranraer and Larne. Amazingly, several decades ago there were plans to build an oil refinery 1 – 2 miles offshore here with a terminal for 50,000 ton tankers to land oil. Common-sense prevailed.

Cashtal yn Ard

Description: well preserved monument nearly as old as
Stonehenge, commanding hill and coastal views: easy,
½ mile
OS map reference: 462892
On the coast road from Laxey (A2) turn left at The
Hibernian onto the A15. After a mile take a right turn
down a narrow road, follow this for about a mile until you
reach a sign on the right for the site. One should be able
to park with care.

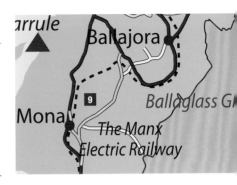

Cashtal yn Ard is 300 yard walk along a clearly signed footpath – this
is the same route that would have been trod by people 4,000 years

ago! Climb over the stone steps to the left of the gate.

Cashtal yn Ard (which translates as 'Castle of the Heights') is on the summit of a plateau with commanding views of the Maughold coast and inland towards North Barrule. It is the site of a Neolithic burial place and is the one of the largest and best preserved of its kind in the British Isles. Archaeologists believe that these ceremonial sites were built by communities in such prominent locations to act as demonstration of their importance to other tribes nearby proclaiming *'this is our place'*. When it was built it was a long barrow (about 130 feet long and 45 feet wide) which was largely covered in stones, earth and grass which has since been stripped away. Believed to have been constructed as a communal burial place for chieftains and their families in the Neolithic period (about 2000BC), it was excavated in the 1930s and in 1999. To put that date in context it is only a few hundred years younger than Stonehenge which has been dated to 2500BC.

At the western end by the kissing gate is the entrance portal of a semi-circle of standing stones, some of which are about 8 feet high and must weigh several tons. Imagine the effort required to transport them to this site. This was long before the appearance of the wheel, so the stones were transported either on wooden sledges or rolled over felled trees. The centre stones lean towards each other creating a narrow and low entrance to the five burial chambers. The entrance to the burial chamber was from the west, symbolically the direction of the setting sun.

The first chamber is noticeably more elongated than the four behind it which are almost square. Beyond the chambers is a low grassed mound where burnt material around a central platform was discovered. This has been interpreted as being a place of cremation. Parallel with chambers are rows of smaller stones running west to east: there are more randomly distributed stones at the eastern edge.

A deed from 1795 names the monument as Cashtal y Muckagh y Vagileragh which translates as 'Castle of the Field Pigsty' – perhaps hinting at its usage before the era when its historical significance was fully appreciated!

There is a similar site, but less well preserved, nearby at Ballafayle. Sites with a common layout to this have been found in Northern Ireland and the west coast of southern Scotland.

Close Sartfield, Ballaugh

Description: lush flower meadows, curraghs show how Island may have looked 15,000 years ago; easy ½ – 1 mile
OS Map Reference: 358956
From the TT Course (A3) turn on to the B9 between Ballaugh and Sulby Glen. Take the third road on the right and follow this for nearly 1 mile. There is a small wooden sign on the right indicating the entrance and car park.

The information board indicates two paths to explore the Manx Wildlife Trust's reserve. The all-season path is a raised walkway taking you by a meadow, through a wetland wooded area (curragh) and ending at a raised bird hide with a delightful panorama. The name Sartfield is derived from the Norse *Svorta vallr* which means swampy field. The summer path takes one through the lush meadows but can be damp if it has rained recently: this is recommended for those more keenly interested in the meadow.

For the all-season path proceed to the end of the car park and through an initial small stretch of boggy woodland. As the last Ice Age ended about 15,000 years ago and the glaciers retreated it is likely that large parts of the Island were very marshy and would have been colonised by vegetation similar to this.

Soon you are walking by the side of an immense wild flower meadow. The countryside was once full of meadows like these bursting with a gorgeous variety of flowering plants, supporting butterflies, insects, farmland birds and other wildlife. However, nearly all of them have been replaced by 'improved grassland' on which it is far more productive to raise cattle. The plethora of flowers is maintained by cutting for hay late in the summer which allows the flowers to re-seed and proliferate. The meadow is at its most abundant from May to July/August: June and into July sees a carpet of orchids in the hay meadows. If you are lucky you may see a rabbit using the tall sward to hide himself.

The walkway turns right when it reaches the fence and the path plunges into the woodland. Here you will see the royal fern, the largest British fern, which does not grow widely on the Island: the more feathery lady fern is the species that predominates. The path ends in a bird hide visited by Prince Charles on Tynwald Day 2000 – I wonder which he enjoyed most, the pageantry and ceremony at St John's or the tranquillity and wildlife here? The splendid view from the hide is over the tops of the trees and encompasses the line of hills ending in North Barrule. Inside are information leaflets on the birds, animals and plants that can be seen in the reserve.

Return to the car park by the same route.

The summer route is marked on the information board and is less well-defined than the all-season one. This is a description of one of the possible walks. Go through the gate and stay close to the fence on the left. The path goes through another gate and skirts round the meadow which gives you a closer view of the plant diversity, and the butterflies that flit between the flowers. In time you will come to a snicket gate whose mechanism includes a horseshoe. Go through this gate, a bridge crosses a ditch and the path takes you snaking through a woodland following small marker posts. The path re-emerges into the meadow which leads back to the car park.

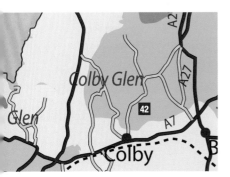

Colby Glen and Ballakilpheric

Description: tranquil wooded glen following the river, option of countryside walk to old hamlet: easy, ½ – 2 miles.
OS map reference: 232709
Follow A27 from Ballasalla, take a right turn a couple of hundred yards past Colby Glen Hotel. Follow the road uphill for half a mile past the first entrance for the glen; just past the second there is a pull-in place where one can park.

Proceed through the gate and down the path towards the river. Cross the river by the footbridge: the glen walk is to the left, the longer countryside walk is straight ahead following the footpath sign. The little pool here is locally known as 'The Fairy Pool'.

The forward footpath takes you to the hamlet of Ballakilpheric which is about a mile away. After a short climb the path levels off with the hedgerows replete with bluebells in the spring. After a moderate climb go through the metal kissing-gate the path continues through open countryside with great views over Castletown, Langness and Ronaldsway Airport. At an old wooden gate the path turns left and soon left again to reach Ballakilpheric – a notable feature of the village is the Victorian chapel. Ballakilpheric is the anglicised version of the Manx *Balley keeill Pharick* which translates as 'the farm of Patrick's church' – the little church is no longer there. Return by the same path, remembering to turn right through the old gate.

For the glen walk go left through the gap in the wall. The glen was purchased by the Government from private ownership in 1955 for £50. Apart from clearing the paths and bridges it is one of the few glens that is not managed by man but left entirely to nature. The land had been owned privately for generations but locals had walked through the glens unchallenged. Then, for a reason not recorded, the owners decided to erect gates to prevent access in 1912. Crowds of locals assembled and took the law into their hands to reinstate their right of way and smashed down the gates. Police were powerless to intervene as the subject of public access to the area was ambiguous. Although on a much bigger scale mass public trespass over Kinder Scout in the Peak District in 1932 eventually lead to establishing the concept of National Parks with free public access over privately owned land.

The path briefly climbs away from the river but then descends by clearly defined steps. The area has a gentle and tranquil charm, especially in the spring and early summer when wild garlic, bluebells and primroses are found in profusion. Pass a closed-off footbridge, you are then directed away from the river by steps and a handrail which afford you views of the countryside. The path then falls away and ends by taking you across the river to meet the road at the lower entrance.

Either take the road back to your vehicle or retrace your steps through the glen.

Cringle Reservoir

Description: walk round reservoir adjoining woodland, back-drop of expansive panorama of the south: easy, ½ mile
OS map reference: 295843
From the A3 Foxdale to Castletown road take the B39 at South Barrule Plantation, there is a car park adjacent to the reservoir.

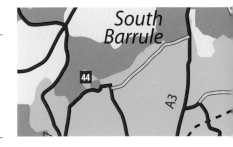

This is an easy walk with views of the Cringle Plantation and South Barrule in one direction and the flat plain around Castletown in the other. The reservoir was built between 1938 and 1946 to supply drinking water to the area to the south. Other reservoirs in the centre of the island took this over in 2008 since when its purpose has been recreational. The reservoir is 35 feet deep and has a capacity of just over 3 million gallons. Cringle Plantation was established in 1958 and is proving to be a good source of timber.

Since 2014 this area has been the site of the annual Granite Mann – the Island's first ever off the road triathlon. It starts with a 400metre swim in Cringle Reservoir, followed by a 10km mountain bike ride along trails through Cringle Plantation ending with a 5km run along the plantation's fire tracks. The distances for each of the three legs are based on those recommended by the British Triathlon Federation. By comparison, today's venture is extremely gentle.

From the left corner follow the path clockwise

round the water's edge. At the top of the reservoir follow the left hand path which briefly takes you away from the water's edge. Bear right after a gentle ascent and follow the footpath sign as it skirts the plantation on your left. Cross over a little bridge with a handrail, you then come to a wall which you keep on your right. The wall is extensively covered in orange lichen – this only grows in areas with little or no pollution, which indicates how clean the air is here. You pass a couple of derelict farm building whose doorway is on the other side from the path. It is likely that this was abandoned when the farmland was flooded to create the reservoir.

The path continues over the retaining wall of the reservoir – the embankment is 70 feet high. The overflow from the reservoir runs into Silverburn River whose glen is well worth a visit

Cronk ny Arrey Laa

Description: short hill walk with awesome coastal cliff views to Calf of Man: easy, ¾ mile.
OS map reference: 232747
Take the A36 and, if you are heading south, park the car on an unmarked road just as the main road takes a sharp left turn.

Walk briefly on the road past the 'Welcome to Rushen' sign and go through a snicket gate on the right to follow the wide clear track straight ahead. It is no time at all before you reach the hilltop. The Ordnance Survey column does not mark the highest elevation, that task is performed by a large cairn a couple of hundred yards further on. This marks a large burial mound dated to Neolithic or early Bronze Age (at least 2500 years ago). For those interested in statistics, Cronk ny Arrey Laa is the 6555th highest peak in the British Isles.

From here there are awesome views of the sea cliff coastline of the south west of the Island extending all the way to the Calf of Man. This is one of the most dramatic views of coastline from any summit, best seen as the sun is sinking in the west. Cronk ny Arrey Laa translates as *'Hill of the day watch'* which references that it was used many centuries ago as a defined look-out station to provide early warning of people approaching the Island by sea. It is also known locally *as Cronk ny Irree-Laa*, meaning hill of the rising day or dawn. It was said that when the sun broke over this hill, it was a sign to the herring-fishers to shoot their nets.

Despite its relatively low altitude compared to the peaks in the north, there are records of three aircraft that have crashed into the hillside. Not only is it very close to sea cliffs that rise suddenly from the sea but also the slopes are often cloaked in mist. Two crashes occurred during the

WW2: one involved a US Airforce plane killing six crewmen on 4th July 1944; another was an RAF plane on a training exercise on 13th November 1944 in which five died. A civilian cargo plane transporting milk from Northern Ireland to Liverpool crashed on 28th September 1948 killing all 4 crew.

A hundred yards west of the cairn (towards the sea) is a Celtic cross, erected in 2000, inscribed with the Manx Fishermen's Hymn which, unfortunately, has been weathered so it is becoming difficult to read. The second verse is particularly stirring:

> Thou, Lord, dost rule the raging of the sea;
> When loud the storm, and furious is the gale,
> Strong is Thine arm; our little barks are frail;
> Send us Thy help; remember Galilee.

Take the same route to descend, ignoring the footpath sign as it does not lead back to where your journey started. Peel is in the distance on the left and in front as far, as the eye can see, is the chain of hills that form the backbone of the Isle of Man.

Dhoon Glen

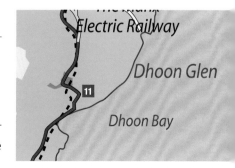

Description: magnificent glen, spectacular waterfall, original art forms on the beach: 1½ miles, steep in places
OS map reference: 453864
Take the coast road (A2) northwards from Laxey until you reach Dhoon Glen Halt (Manx Electric Railway). There is ample parking in the lay-by opposite the refreshment hut.

Dhoon Glen (*Glion y Dowin* in Manx) runs for ¾ mile

through a wooded valley following a stream to Dhoon Bay. It is one of the steepest glens with a descent of 560 feet (170 metres) with over 190 steps back, but it amply rewards one's effort. Jenkinson wrote in his tour guide in 1874 *"They are undoubtedly the largest and most beautiful cascades on the island, but hitherto they have been very little known. They are deeply recessed in a romantic and well-wooded glen"*. There is no reason to dispute this description.

Cross the MER line to the hut and immediately to its right there are concrete steps leading down past public conveniences to join a path that goes by the side of the stream. There is flight of steps down, then a wooden walkway and another short flight of steps. The path passes under a bridge and reaches a section with a wooden handrail

(Alternatively one can take the minor road a few hundred yards and just beyond the Raad ny Foillan waymarker there is a gate and footpath sign for Dhoon Beach. The path heads left downhill through trees to reach a wooden fence/hand rail).

Turn right downhill following the handrail for the best views of the valley and stream below. As this comes to an end proceed down the path that is slightly away from the edge. Pick your way carefully as the surface can be a bit uneven and muddy as it is used by rainwater rivulets. The path heads uphill briefly towards the remains of a chimney and a building which housed a large wheel that pumped water out of the lead and tin mine here in mid-19th century.

The mine was never profitable and In 1872 William Quilleash, who owned the Dhoon, sold a large amount of the land to William Bailie and leased the upper part of the glen, including the waterfall, to James Quilleash of Oregon, USA. James Quilleash began to develop the glen for visitors and by the early 1880s his site boasted refreshment rooms, stabling and the Dhoon Waterfall Inn. Perhaps in rivalry to this, Bailie built Dhoon Glen Hotel on the site that is now the car park and a restaurant down on the shore. By the late 1880s 50,000 people were visiting the glen.

The *Manx Fairy*, a small passenger ship, used to run daily between Douglas and Ramsey calling at Dhoon Bay to unload passengers, who spent the day on the beach or in the glen, before being picked up for the return journey. With the arrival of the Isle of Man Electric Tramway in 1897 the glen was taken over by the company who charged 4d admission of which the owners received 1 3/4d. Its popularity waned after the Second World War and the Forestry Board purchased the glen in 1955 for £2,000 – a fraction of what it was valued at 60 years previously

Proceed along the path and at a bench it forks, take the left branch where there are steps down for close-up views of the waterfalls. The first part is the smaller section where water tumbles over the rocks with views upstream of trees that have fallen over and now act as small bridges. The path hugs the side of the stream and through gaps in the trees you begin to notice the Irish Sea in the distance. Ferns and mosses cover the cliffs on the right giving it a carpet-like feel as you brush your hand against it.

As the sound of the rushing water grows in volume you come to a T-junction – take the left path and zig-zagging down you begin to see a second, taller section of the waterfall. (The right path is an old pack horse track – a higher level route which by-passes the second part of the waterfall and joins the main trail lower down the valley). It is known as the *Inneen Vooar* or 'Big Girl' and is one of the highest on the Island falling over 130 feet (40 metres) in the two drops. In miniature this waterfall is the equal of those you might see in travel programmes that take you through tropical paradises. Back to the Isle of Man, and in Manx folklore there is a story of a young girl having been drowned in the pool below the waterfall, and it is said that her ghost haunts the glen.

Cross an old stone bridge so the stream is now on your right. There are now a succession of modern bridges which snakes the path from one side of the river to the other and back – the Forestry Division have clearly invested heavily in making this part of the glen accessible to walkers.

The path spills out onto Dhoon Beach and in the distance, on a clear day, you can make out the Lakeland fells. On my visit some person or people had balanced flat stones and pebbles on top of each other on the beach to create over twenty mini towers some as tall as three feet. The overall effect is a wonderful display of spontaneous popular art.

Return by the same route.

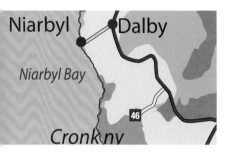

Eary Cushlin and Lag ny Keeilley

Description: grassland and clifftop walk in remote and peaceful spot, ancient chapel (keeill): easy to Eary Cushlin, moderate to steep beyond, ½ – 2½ miles
OS map reference: 225762
Take A27 from Peel, 2 miles south of Dalby turn right down minor road which passes Kerroodhoo Plantation, at the end of which is a car park.

Proceed through the kissing gate and follow the broad track downhill towards Eary Cushlin. This used to be a farm, originally used only seasonally, which was acquired by the Government in 1957: it is now an outdoor activity centre. Here, and for the rest of the walk, are breathtaking views of the coastal cliffs to the south ending at The Calf of Man. The summit above is Cronk ny Arrey Laa which translates as '*Hill of the day watch*'. There are many such locations on the Island dating back at least 500 years when residents of each parish were tasked with keeping a watch, both during day and night, for potential enemies approaching the Island by sea.

Beyond Eary Cushlin the track crosses a narrow stream with stepping stones and becomes a moderately sloping footpath. One passes a sign indicating that this footpath crosses rough terrain for a mile heading towards the early Christian keeill. The path crosses the route of the Coastal Footpath (*Raad ny Foillan*), but continues straight ahead. After a short time one passes a bench on the left where one can rest to appreciate what is one of the remotest locations on the entire Island. And on a clear day one can glimpse the Mountains of Mourne in Northern Ireland. If you are not up for the more

challenging path ahead this is a good place to turn back.

Onwards certain parts of the path can be a little boggy and from late summer onwards bracken can obscure the route in places. The path crosses through a gap in the stone wall on two occasions and there is a very brief scramble over rocks. The last few hundred yards to the keeill is steeply sloping.

The keeill was built in the 8th century on a natural flat ledge in otherwise sloping area – the Manx name for the site is Lag ny Keeilley which translates from Manx to 'The Hollow of the Chapel'. One does wonder why such a remote and not easily accessible site was chosen for a place of worship. Certainly the itinerant priest who made his way here would probably feel much closer to God in such a location. And his congregation more pious for making the journey here.

Like all keeills, it was orientated with the altar facing east towards the Holy Land while the entrance faced west. The priest would preach to his congregation, who stood outside, from the doorway. The keeill was small, inside about 12 feet by 9 feet, which allowed only for the priest to worship there. Numerous white quartz pebbles are found near the keeill which may be associated with people saying a prayer for, or remembering, the dead who are buried here – this was used as a graveyard into the 19th century. The priest slept in a small separate building and was probably dependant on his congregation for food and drink.

Spend a few minutes in quiet contemplation before you return along the same path.

Earystane Nature Reserve, Colby

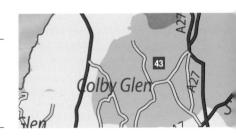

Description: stroll through woodland and curragh wetland, a hide for birdwatching: easy, ½ mile.
OS map reference: 235715
Take the A27 northwards at Colby. After 1½ miles the road bends sharp right by a sign for Earystane and on the left 150 yards along the road there is a pull-in place.

The site of Earystane was originally part of Ballachrink (translates from Manx Gaelic to 'Hill farm') and was sold to Arbory Parish Commissioners and used as a tip until the 1980s. In 1996 Manx Wildlife Trust was awarded a grant by Barclays to turn the tip into a nature reserve and public amenity. The part of the site that was used for tipping has been colonised by grassland. The wetter, lower lying part of the site was not used for this purpose and now willows grow there.

At the junction of the main and minor roads proceed through the gate and immediately a wooded path stretches in front of you. Walk through a tunnel formed by a variety of trees: in spring this is carpeted with flowers. The grassland area on the left is managed as small hay

meadow with the vegetation being cut in late summer after the wild flowers have set seed for the next year. Prior to this it can look overgrown. In the spring and summer the fields above are full of sheep. On the left is a hide which looks out over the curragh (marshy woodland) and surrounding countryside. There are information notices on the walls listing the birds that have been spotted here.

Beyond the hide follow the path down onto the raised wooden walkway. This takes one on a short circuit through the curragh itself. The wetland is dominated by grey willow and supports a diversity of woodland and wetland plants such as ground ivy, bluebells, marsh marigold, rushes and orchids.

Elfin Glen and Albert Tower

Description: woodland walk between two famous TT landmarks, separate path to Albert Tower, great views of Ramsey and the north: moderate with occasional steep section, 2 miles
OS map reference: 449934
Take the Mountain Road (A18) out of Ramsey, there is parking on the outside of Ramsey Hairpin.

Originally called Ballacowle Glen in it was given the English name, Elfin Glen, in mid 19th century to attract holidaymakers. Proceed up the wooden steps, turn left at the top and in 20 yards turn right by the footpath sign. There is a short, sharp climb uphill to start with, the path bears left and the ascent becomes gentler. At the three point sign carry forward towards the Gooseneck, you can take the other path to Albert Tower on the way down. The path is bisected by drainage culverts that carries run-off from the TT Course. Ignore the gap in the wall and the path on the right as you keep going forwards. The path leaves the cover of woodland and becomes more grassed over with ferns on either side. The slopes of North Barrule start appearing in front of you. Cross a short wooden walkway, then up a few stone steps and you are out on the Mountain Road. The Gooseneck itself is a couple of hundred yards away on the left.

Retrace your steps downhill until you reach the footpath sign for Albert Tower. It was built to commemorate the visit of Prince Albert in 1847. He climbed to the top of the hill lead by the town's barber, who was pressed into action as a guide at short notice, and was followed by a crowd of curious locals (the royal party's arrival was totally unexpected). From the summit, which was thereafter named Albert Mount, he viewed the town of Ramsey and the northern plain. His wife, Queen Victoria, remained on-board the royal yacht moored in the bay where she met the Bishop. The tower is well worth the half mile walk,

but bear in mind there is a brief steep stretch.

The path goes through a metal gate past a footpath sign on a tree going right uphill, rather than left on the flat. The path becomes moderately steep through the trees. It flattens off as it leaves the woodland and you see a mobile phone mast which is clad in plastic vegetation in an attempt to obscure it from view. The path continues level and straight as Albert Tower comes into view.

Dramatic views open up of Ramsey Bay, the sandy beach stretching northwards for miles and the northern plain with the villages of Jurby, Andreas and Bride. Conveniently a bench has been provided to enable you to enjoy the panorama. The path continues with views on your right of North Barrule and the ribbon-like Mountain Road. The tower is 45 feet high and made from slate and granite but, unfortunately, it is not usually open. The now fading plaque reads 'Erected on the spot where HRH Prince Albert stood to view Ramsey and its neighbourhood during the visit of Her Most Gracious Majesty , Queen Victoria to Ramsey Bay on XXth September MDCCCLVII'. On the far side there are views east to Maughold Head and, on a clear day, over to the Lakeland Fells.

Return to the car park by retracing the route that you took earlier.

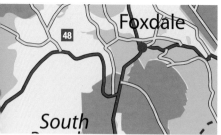

Foxdale Mines

Description: historic industrial buildings in rugged, bleak upland setting: easy, 1 mile
OS map reference: 295843
Take A36 from South Barrule Forest Park and turn first right and park near the derelict mine tower.

There is a gate on the right giving entry to the disused mine workings – signs indicate the need for caution when walking. The tall tower immediately in front is part of the Cross Vein mine, popularly known as Snuff the Wind due to its exposed location, which was worked, primarily for lead, for 50 years from the 1830s.

Mining on the Island was at its peak from the 1850s to the 1890s producing up to 20% of the total GB output of zinc and 5% of its lead – the majority of the latter coming from the mines here. Several hundred would have been employed at the Foxdale mines. Many would have lived in the surrounding villages and hamlets and would have had an hour's walk to the mine shaft entrance followed by a vertical climb down hundreds of feet of wooden ladders – only to be repeated in reverse after a 10 or 12 hour shift underground. By the end of the working of the mines the lowest levels were nearly 2,000 feet in depth. The waste heaps

were known as 'deads' because they contained traces of lead which contaminated the area and made it a struggle for vegetation to survive.

Behind these buildings you will see further evidence of mine workings in the distance – this is known as Dixon's Vein. Walk along a track across the heather bearing slightly to your right. The track crosses over a stream and heads towards the two sets of buildings. The fencing round the one on the right has fallen down so one can carefully pick your way through the remains for a close up view of the building. There are hearths at both ends and what looks like a deep, narrow trench in the middle. It is believed that this might have been used as a sheep dip by hill farmers who used the land when the mines closed.

There is a large rectangle of low stones assembled into a wall, most of which are grassed over, which surrounds the building. These look to be from an earlier age than the mine, possibly when this area was farmed and the wall enclosed a vegetable garden keeping the livestock out. It is possible that many stones were taken from the wall to construct the miner's huts.

Return to the Cross Vein mine and take the left road, indicated as a dead end, to the more extensive Beckwith mine. Mining of Beckwith's Vein started in the 1840s when it was described as one of the largest ore bodies ever discovered in Britain. The gate is locked but the derelict buildings are easy to pick out across the spoil heaps.

Garey Ny Cloie, St John's

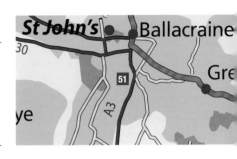

Classification: the most varied woodland on the entire Island – Global Tree Trail: easy, ¾ mile.
OS map reference: 280812
Garey ny Cloie is situated on the A40 close to its junction with the A3, about half a mile south of Tynwald Hill. Parking facilities are near the main gate to the grounds of the Government offices.

For many decades this woodland garden has been the headquarters for Government's forestry operations. In the early 1960s, during major renovation works, much of the presently maturing woodland was established. The site is bounded to the west by the route of the old St John's to Foxdale railway branch line and the slopes of Slieau Whallian in the east. There is a rifle range to the south. The Foxdale River which flows through Garey ny Cloie before joining the Neb which flows to Peel.

The site is laid out over several acres and there is a feeling of peace and tranquillity: there is much to reward those interested in trees and shrubs usually associated with grandiose gardens. There are 42 different tree species from Europe, America and Asia with many less common ones including Indian horse chestnut, maidenhair tree, copper beech and hybrid southern beech. The trees are marked with a number which refer to details in the leaflets that are available near the car park.

There are several trails through the woodlands. In springtime the shrub borders of evergreen azalea, dwarf rhododendron and camellia provide added colour and diversity to an already varied collection of Japanese flowering cherry trees.

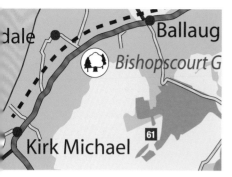

Glen Dhoo

Description: remote countryside walk, utterly tranquil, historic farm buildings: easy, 1 mile.

OS map reference: 352919

Take the TT Course (A3) to Ballaugh. Immediately after hump back bridge turn right by the Raven pub and follow the minor road for a mile. The road steepens and the surface becomes a little uneven for a couple of hundred yards and you reach a parking area by the entrance to Ballaugh plantation.

Walk back down the road until you come to a Greenway track sign for Bayr Glas on the left. The track climbs gently and in a couple of hundred yards you will start to see the wooded slopes of the hills that surround the valley. You walk past bright yellow coconut-scented gorse and primroses and bluebells in the spring. The path rises and falls but never steeply so.

On the right you pass a 4 foot high vertical slate with hole which was probably the gatepost of the farm that lies further along. The path can become a little muddy for a few yards as a small brook crosses over to the main stream. Proceed through two gates, the second of which marks the entrance to the Manx Nature Conservation Trust Reserve. Glen Dhoo means black or dark glen, which is appropriate when late in the day Slieau Curn casts its shadow.

Cross the stream by the stepping stones, or the large slate slab, over to the abandoned farmhouse (known as a *tholtan* in Manx) where there is an information board. It is a two-storey building with dating back to the 18th century with a hearth at either end: it is quite a grand building for such a relatively remote location. The area around here is known as The Port or The Phurt (probably translates from Manx as 'boggy ground') where there was once a group of 10 buildings. In 1841 Census this is

recorded as a thriving community comprising farmers, a weaver, a nailer, a wool spinner and a tailor – although it is likely that the men supplemented the household income by fishing in the summer. The last person to have lived here left in the early 1920s.

Continue along the grassy path past more examples of derelict farm buildings and walls (many now grassed over). On the left there is a rusted wheel which indicates that there was a small water mill here: traces of the mill race (channel) and mill pond can be seen. Climb over the stile to pass further old structures – the building on the right, with a massive tree trunk leaning against it, is quite substantial.

This is a good place pause and absorb how isolated it must have been living here before turning around and retracing your steps.

Glen Helen

Description: walk through varied and scenic woodland by river running through deep gorge, waterfall: easy, 1½ miles
OS map reference: 295843
There is a car park at the, now closed, Glen Helen Inn (just after Glen Helen 2) on TT Course (A3) two miles north of Ballacraine.

Perhaps the best known of the Island's glens, Glen Helen was created in the 1860s by a consortium of Manx businessmen who laid its paths, carried out extensive planting of trees and ornamental shrubs and constructed river bridges. It was opened to the public in 1867 for a small charge (originally four pence). It was originally known as *Glen* Rhenass, the name of the river flowing through it, but was re-named after a lady in the life of the then owner John Marsden. It was subsequently taken over by the Manx Government in 1958. There is a variety of impressive trees including sequoia, thuja, spruces, Douglas fir, oak, sycamore and beech which give a beautiful variegated appearance for the walk.

Proceed along the tarmac road past the Swiss House restaurant and on the right you can see the children's playground, nearby is the restored fountain which is nearly 150 years old. In 1933 the famous lady flyer Amy Johnson visited the glen and to mark the occasion she planted a Douglas fir, which is adjacent to the fountain. The main path keeps the river on your right – one can cross over by bridge but certain stretches of the path on this side were closed at the time of writing. Given the steep sides of the valley and the tall trees some of their crowns are almost 200 feet above you. In dramatic fashion a few trees have fallen over across the river. The path is relatively wide and is in good condition: gradually it takes you higher from the river which provides some wonderful views.

There is a bridge over a small stream at the Rhenass Waterfall. After stopping to admire the spectacle continue on up a short flight of stone steps. Just beyond the handrail take the stepped path on the left and proceed towards the wooden railings. You are now directly above the main waterfall which you can hear but not see. Walk round a little further and you can see a torrent of water rushing on its way between the rocks.

Retrace the path to return to the car park. Towards the end cross the bridge to see close up the 50 foot sheer rock face by the children's playground.

Glen Maye

Description: woodland walk through profusely vegetated glen to a beach, dramatic waterfall: easy, occasionally moderate, 1 mile
OS map reference: 236798
On A27 road south from Peel, use car park by the Waterfall Inn in Glen Maye village

In 1960 the glen was purchased by the Forestry Board from the owner of the Waterfall Inn who had been charging an entrance fee of 3d. Like all National Glens entrance is now free. At the time of writing the Waterfall Inn was closed.

The original name for Glen Maye was *Glion* Muigh which translates as 'Yellow Glen'. This recognised that when the river flooded it brought down iron residue from the surrounding hills which turned the water yellow (or yellowy brown). The entrance to the glen is at the bottom of the car park down a flight of steps: there are public toilets on the right.

The sound of rushing water soon hits your ears as it throws itself down narrow channels and falls headlong over the rocks. The waterfall (*Spooty Vooar*) is said to be the home of the Buggane – the Manx version of the bogey-man. The Buggane is a mischief maker invariably depicted as a large, often ugly creature. It can appear in any shape it

pleases – as an ogre with a huge head and great fiery eyes; as a small dog which grows larger and larger as you watch it; as horned monster or anything it chooses. Each Buggane has his own particular dwelling-place.

Pause on the bridge over the river to look downstream towards the steep cliffs which can often hide this glen completely from sunlight. Use the path that closely follows the course of the river, the return will be by the higher level route which are the turnings on the left. Take the second wooden walkway to have a good view of the vegetation covered cliff face and waterfall which plunges beneath you.

The path is now gentler, and some stretches are concreted, but the river continues to be dynamic. The very damp microclimate enables a variety of ferns and other plants to flourish. After a while the river widens and becomes more peaceful. The riverside path briefly goes uphill by a flight of steps but climbs down to follow the water. A bridge takes you over the river so it is now on your left.

On the right is the remains of the building that used to house a waterwheel which pumped water out of a small mine that was operational from the 1740s until the 1870s (known as 'The Mona Erin'). Lead was extracted but it was poor quality. If you walk round and peer through the archway you can appreciate how long, narrow and tall the building was in order to house the water wheel.

A gate leads you onto a minor road which you follow downhill – you now have an aerial view of the wheelhouse. As you pass over a footbridge the sea comes into view, the cliffs now tower above you. Follow the path down to the shingle beach. The coves around here are said to have been used for smuggling in the 17th century.

Return the way you came back to the gate that leads into the glen then back over the bridge. This time follow the signs for the upper path which affords a different view of the river as it is now 50 – 60 feet below you. The path is wide, flat and easy to negotiate and eventually returns you to the first bridge that you crossed when you entered the glen.

Glen Wyllin and Cooildarry

Classification: woodland walk and Nature Reserve, dramatic river cliffs, rounded off with a stroll to the coast: easy, 1½ miles.
OS map reference: 313903
Follow TT course (A3), immediately before entering Kirk Michael there is a sharp left turn signposted Peel (A4). Take this road for 300 yards and take a right turn into Glen Wylin. There is parking either just before the tall brick structures (supports for an old railway bridge) or after.

This area was opened to the public as the Glen Wyllin Pleasure Grounds in 1890. The glen was a thriving attraction for several decades offering a range of amusements for a three pence charge for adults. It was acquired by the Isle of Man Railway Company in 1935 and continued as a successful tourist attraction until the 1950s. It fell into disrepair and was acquired by the Forestry Board in 1978. Glen Wyllin translates into English as 'Glen of the mill'.

Start from the gravel parking area just before the old railway bridge support tower, follow the wooden rail towards the woodland and, at the end, turn left to take a path that runs along the edge of the trees. Keep to the low level path, climb a flight of steps and cross the road carefully. Just to the right of the road sign is a Manx Wildlife Trust footpath which could be muddy in places if it has been raining recently (see alternative approach). The path passes behind cottages and skirts woodland whose floor is carpeted with bluebell, primrose, wood anemone and wild garlic in the spring. There is an abundance of rhododendron that flowers later in the year. There is a small footbridge as the path crosses a wider track: pause at the information board before you enter Cooildarry Nature Reserve.

An alternative approach to the Reserve is to follow the narrow road on the left of the path. This becomes a Greenway track which leads up to the Nature Reserve entrance and information board.

On the left there are spectacular views down to the Cooil Dharry river, the path descends to bring you closer to the water. There are a wide variety of trees including elm, ash, sycamore, beech, oak and sweet chestnut many of which have been planted in the last 30-40 years. Take a wooden bridge across the river and follow the left path going uphill – we will explore the lower path on the way back. You pass a tumbling waterfall near the site of the Fuller's Earth works which date from the 1830s. You might see some rusted machinery among the bushes on the right and a derelict mill is on the left. Fuller's Earth is a calcium-based clay that is fine, off-white, and highly absorbent. It was extracted from the earth in this area and used as an important ingredient in absorbing and removing oil from sheep's wool. It is also used as an inert substance in artillery shells.

The path climbs away from the river through a profusion of wild garlic in spring. It finishes by a gate which leads on to the main road. Return the way you have come but just before the wooden bridge take a sharp left to follow the path by the river that was mentioned earlier. Across the river is a very tall bank which indicates the extent that the river has eroded the land since the end of the last Ice Age about 15,000 years ago. Follow the path across two bridges and after a flight of steps you are now on top of the bank that you saw earlier. The path snakes down to the river which is on your right and re-joins the one that you were on earlier. Leave the Nature Reserve by the gate and return taking the path on the left through the trees and across the road.

As a bonus, venture along road through Glen Wylin campsite to its end by the sea. The sea cliffs here are made of blown sand and are easily eroded by stormy seas. Man has attempted to halt this by using huge concrete blocks and granite boulders as protection. However, the effect is simply to concentrate the erosion further down the coast where it is not protected. Kirk Michael is slowly losing its coastline which threatens the safety of nearby housing. However, don't dwell on that but enjoy the view on the left back to Peel with Corrin's Tower on top of the hill and on the right up the coast to Jurby and, on a clear day, the outline of the Galloway Hills in southern Scotland.

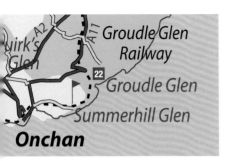

Groudle Glen

Description: coast and glen walk, with several delights including steam railway, waterwheel and a wizard: easy, 1 mile

OS map reference: 420784

From the northern end of Douglas Promenade take A11 following the Manx Electric Railway. Turn right down Groudle Old Road, also signed Groudle Cottages, and park in the car park at the foot of the hill.

In 1890 an entrepreneur, Richard Maltby Broadbent, purchased the lease to the whole area here. He determined to landscape it, build a hotel and other facilities to transform it into a major tourist attraction. There are three different and interesting experiences to be had here – Groudle Bay, the miniature steam railway and the glen walk itself. Today you will have a trip to the North Pole, see a miniature version of the Laxey Wheel and have an encounter with Gandalf.

From the car park take the path towards to Port Groudle beach with the river on your left. The beach has been formed by the continuous action of storm tides that bring up pebbles and rocks from the sea bed and hurl them up to form the bank. The shape of the beach is changing constantly in response to the power of the sea. During periods of high tide one can see waves heading upstream, seemingly against the flow of the river, up to and beyond the bridge.

Retrace your steps and cross the river on the wooden bridge and follow the steps up the slope to approach the railway track and a stop named North Pole Halt. The Groudle Glen Railway, 2 foot gauge, was originally built in 1896 to attract visitors and transport them to man-made pools which housed sea lions and polar bears. Indeed 100,000

visitors were attracted to the glen at the peak of its popularity. The railway fell into disrepair in the 1960s. In 1982 volunteers started work on the railway and it was re-opened to the public in 1986. It is operates on Sundays from April to October with occasional evening services in the summer. Outside these times one can walk alongside the track beyond the Halt along the cliff top towards the Sea Lion Rocks Terminus. Beyond this one can see the remains of an open air pool which used to house polar bears and sea lions until early in 20th century.

On the left of the North Pole Halt by the blue footpath sign there is a flight of steps down to a path that skirts the woods and leads you into the glen itself. On the right is a huge tank which has been creatively painted to try to blend in with the surrounding trees. The path along the glen is relatively flat and even with the river on your left. Originally referred to as 'The Fern Land of Mona', the glen was developed by planting many different types of trees (not necessarily ones that would grow naturally in this location). By side of the path a tree has been carved to represent Gandalf from Lord of the Rings.

After a few minutes you will see a path on the right leading up to the Lhen Coan Station. The station is attractively designed and has advertising signs from a bygone era when Bermaline bread 'gratified and satisfied' and Okell's Pale Ale was 'the equal of the finest imported beers'. Beyond the end of the tracks there is a path going up to the top of the glen and eventually leading on to the main road. This gives some wonderful views down to the stream and the occasional waterfall.

For the main glen walk return down the steps to the river and cross the bridge. This path continues for another mile. It is worth venturing a little further to see a couple of attractions. There used to be a bandstand which has been rebuilt on the site only much smaller. A little further you can see a water wheel known as the "Little Isabella" (a reference to the Laxey Wheel named Lady Isabella). It was built in 1894 with the original purpose of pumping water up to the Groudle Hotel which was on the main road. Whether it served this purpose or was just ornamental is open to conjecture.

At the time of writing the river bank here was fenced off but the path beyond the wheel was open. The gorge noticeably narrows and the sound of rushing water becomes louder. Soon you will see an impressive viaduct towering over the glen. The viaduct which is 130 feet long was originally built so that the Manx Electric Railway could extend beyond Groudle to Laxey.

At this point the adventurous can extend their walk through the glen for another ¾ mile by continuing straight on under the viaduct. However, severe flooding in the winter of 2015-16 caused some parts of the path to be damaged or obstructed so this section may not be easy to complete. If you take the path that hairpins left you will very soon reach the top entrance to the glen. Across the road is Groudle Station where trains still stop to bring people to the glen from Douglas, as they did over one hundred years ago. However, the Groudle Hotel that was here no longer exists. From here you can follow the main road left back down to the turning for Groudle Beach. Or you can return to the car park by the riverside path that you have just walked.

Kerrowdhoo and Clypse Reservoirs

Description: walk round two picturesque reservoirs on the edge of countryside: easy, 1 mile
OS Map reference: 400807
Take the Mountain Road (A18) to Hilberry, 36 mile marker, then turn off taking the Ballacottier Road and Clypse Moar Road (signposted Clypse and Conrhenny Walks) to the Clypse-e-Creer car park.

Walk downhill along the road between the hedgerow banks which in spring are covered in yellow primroses. The road goes through a gate by the reservoir keeper's house. There is an information board on the right.

Follow the path down on the right towards the Kerrowdhoo Reservoir which is the lower of the two reservoirs and was built in 1893. It is the larger of the two with a surface area of 11.6 acres and a depth of 40 feet. It can hold about 50 million gallons of water. The channel on the left is the overflow from the Clypse Reservoir above. Cross over the bridge and choose between a clockwise or anticlockwise circuit. The small pond on the left is sometimes home to young families of coots (black with white beak), moorhens (red beaks) or ducks. At the dam wall at the far end one can appreciate the depth of the valley in which the reservoir sits. There is a wooden hide and benches on the reservoir's edge. The reservoirs are a good place for fishing as they are stocked regularly with rainbow and brown trout.

The Clypse Reservoir is the upper of two reservoirs and was built in 1876 as Douglas was expanding due to the boom in tourism. The

surface is 6.3 acres and has a depth of 40 feet with an overall capacity of around 32 million gallons. In 1954 Clypse Course (10.8 miles) was adopted for Lightweight 125 & Sidecar TT races instead of the Mountain Course as it was less prone to delays due to adverse weather. It passes about half a mile to the east of the reservoir. It did not prove popular with competitors and these races reverted to the TT Course in 1960.

Again make your own choice about the direction of your walk. The shallow pond at the far end has bushes right down to the water which makes if very suitable place for ducks to bring up their young. The fields around the Clypse are often home to retired heavy working horses.

King Orry's Grave, Laxey

Description: famous pre-historic monument, bisected by politician's home: easy, ¼ mile
OS map reference: 438843
Located in Minorca near the village of Laxey where the B11 crosses the A2 (road between Douglas and Ramsey).

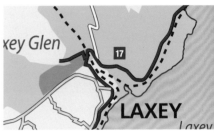

In the middle of the 19th century the bones of several humans together with the skeleton of a horse were found which gave rise to the tale that the site was the grave of King Orry. King Orry, properly known as King Godred of Crovan, had taken control of the Isle of Man and many of the islands between it and Norway in 1079. He and his descendants ruled the Island for the next two centuries – albeit not continuously. However, there is no connection between this historical figure and these Neolithic remains.

The pre-historic monument, known in Manx as *Gretch Veg*, now comprises two structures separated by a road: but originally it was a single extensive ceremonial and burial site. It dates from the Neolithic era, perhaps 4,000-3,000 years ago. The site was built by the people who lived nearby as a memorial to their ancestors – its location on a hill would mean that it would have been clearly visible for some distance. Indeed, it only in the last 100 years or so that the village has grown around it meaning that it no longer dominates the surrounding countryside. Ceremonies would have been held on the site at different times of the year.

The area higher up the road has more of its original stones in place. It comprises a forecourt of 12 yards across and 4 yards deep and contains three chambers once filled with the remains of many dead bodies. The chambers would have been 'roofed' with rocks and turf but this has long since gone. The lower site has an open cist 'grave' – a square stone box (measuring approx. 3 feet by 2 feet) into which a dead body was placed in a crouch or foetal position. It has a single standing stone about 8 feet tall which is called a portal-stone and would have been one of an arc of stones. The house between the two sites is the home of the President of Tynwald.

Information boards provide descriptions of the construction and use of the sites.

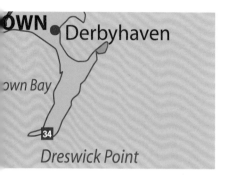

Langness

Description: coast and heathland walk, very varied scenery in such a short walk: easy, 1- 1½ miles
OS map reference: 285660
Just before you enter Castletown on A5 from Douglas take the first left at the roundabout to Derbyhaven on A12. On passing the Airport perimeter turn right towards the golf course and in 400 yards take a right turn down a narrow road that threads its way across the golf course. There is a car park at the very end of this road by the Private sign.

Langness comes from the Norse word for 'long promontory'. This is an Area of Special Scientific Interest (ASSI) due to saltmarsh and coastal heath which provides habitats for many species of wildlife and plants. Over the four seasons twenty different types of birds call the area their home – several use it as their wintering place before they migrate in the spring.

Turn left from the car park and follow the blue Raad ny Foillan signed

path by the edge of the low cliffs. Straight in front over the water you can see the Calf of Man and, a little detached from this, the Chicken Rock lighthouse. On your right you can see the loosely compacted Conglomerate rock which has been eroded by the sea to form inlets and arches. Keep the fence on your left. At the corner of the field the main path curves left and there is a smaller one on the right. At low tide it is possible to scramble over the rocks to the first and second of the Skerrans, although the third is inaccessible. You will come across derelict walls which marks the site of a former fort.

The main path continues left to the corner of the lighthouse: by the sea you can see a small landing stage that may have been built to unload the herring boats. The lighthouse was built in 1880 using limestone quarried from Castletown. Follow the path through the gate as it circles the wall of the lighthouse. Jeremy Clarkson used to live in the building but, in 2012 he decided to vacate it when the path that you are on was officially recognised as a Public Right of Way. He was rather peeved that people were able to peer into his kitchen. The building is now self-catering holiday accommodation. Like the lighthouse, the Dreswick Harbour foghorn is no longer operative. Dreswick is derived from the Norse *Drangsvik* meaning the creek in the rocks. Grey seals can be seen her basking on the rocks. You are at the most southerly point on the Isle of Man.

At this point one can either return the way that you came or continue round towards the tower in the centre of the peninsular. To do the latter proceed through the gate and take the path on the right across the grass.

The narrow inlets on the right are often referred to as gullets. In 1925 a whale came ashore alive onto the beach of one of these. Its length (48 feet) meant that it was unable to turn around and head back to sea and so was stranded when the tide went out. Its body was towed out by boat to Derbyhaven Bay, from where it was transported behind three steam traction engines to Douglas. The cleaned skeleton is on display at the Manx Museum.

The tower has a precarious spiral stair case inside leading to the top from which, it is alleged, a beacon was lit to guide the herring fleet home. The Ordnance Survey trig point nearby is one of the lowest on the Isle of Man – less than 100 feet above sea level.

Carry on along the wide path for a few hundred yards until you come across a small building. It has an outer and an inner wall which is typical of buildings used to store explosives – if an accident happened two walls were better than one to contain the blast. A few yards beyond the building the path goes through a gap in the wall, follow a cleared path through the grass on your left and you can now easily see the car park.

Laxey Glen Gardens

Description: picturesque glen walk through a former
pleasure garden: easy, 1 mile
OS map reference: 431843
The glen is located in Laxey on the main coast road (A2):
immediately after the bridge by the Laxey Flour Mill there
is a turning on the left which leads up to a car park.

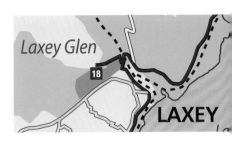

This area started to be actively managed in 1800 when the Reverend
William Fitzsimmons began a planting programme. Some of the larger
trees in the glen date from this period. To capitalise on the boom in
tourism the Glen Gardens was opened as a public leisure area known
as Victoria Park in the 1860s – it accommodated a host of attractions
and a pavilion. The Gardens were an extensive visitor attraction judging
by this description in 1881 *'containing, among other attractions and
amusements, pleasant and secluded walks, bowers, and rustic seats,
swings, quoits, and hobby horses, croquet, lawn tennis, bowling green,
American bowling saloon, and everything needful to enable visitors to
spend a most enjoyable day'*. A decline in tourist numbers resulted in
the glen being sold to the Forestry Board in 1956.

Follow the road past the Laxey Pavilion which houses a café. Take
the path into the glen itself: on your left is a flat rectangular lawn was
originally used for croquet or bowling. Continue on the right path which
follows the direction of the valley in which the Glen Roy flows. It hairpins
down to, and crosses, the river which is now on your right. The path
follows the river uphill through the trees, notice a log which has been
carved into the shape of a crocodile.

Keep on the path close to the river – its sound, as much as its
appearance, is rewarding.
After a while you
encounter a low wall on
either side of the path
which appears to create a
channel for water
elevated above the course
of the river. The path
becomes a little more
challenging to walk and is
the opportunity to take
stock of where you are
and make a decision to
return. But enjoy the
delight of the small
waterfall on the right
before you do so.

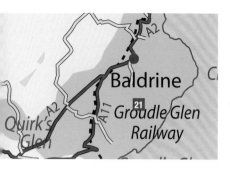

Lonan Old Church

Description: historic church in remote setting, arguably the smallest in use on the Island: easy, ¼ mile
OS map reference: 427784
Take the A2 from Douglas towards Laxey. A few hundred yards past the Liverpool Arms turn right by a bus shelter down a minor road signed Lonan Old Church. Take the second left turn (after half a mile) signed St Adamnan's Church and park off the road.

The church is officially known as St Adamnan, which translates as *Little Adam*: he was an Irish saint of the 7th century.

A keeill (an early Christian chapel) has existed on this site since the middle of the 7th century, and possibly a smaller religious building was here from the middle of the 5th century. It is alleged that from 447AD Christian missionaries started arriving from Ireland. They were Celtic Christians, rather than from the Church of Rome, and they were organised differently – for instance, their monasteries could comprise men and women who could marry and raise children. Those wanting a more spiritual life could live alone within the local community. These holy men were known as Culdees and each would build a small chapel (called a cabbal) with a priest's cell attached. Cabbals were only small so it is likely that the priest would administer to his congregation outside. The later keeill would have been slightly larger and would have had a window, which the cabbals lacked.

The open section of the current building dates from 12th century, when the church was owned by the Prior of St Bee's Abbey in Cumberland, and is unchanged. Just to the right of the archway entrance there is a small hole in the brick wall, known as the leper slant, through which beggars could view the Mass and be given alms. Inside the church, which was completely restored between 1895 and 1897, is little more than 20 feet long, but it houses several rows of pews together with a raised altar area and an organ.

The church remains here only by luck or laziness. It is located at a remote corner of the parish of Lonan which it served. In the 19th century parishioners, who were tired of the long walk to the church from their farmsteads, persuaded the authorities to build a new church in a more central location. (The existing church had actually been built adjacent to the old packhorse route from Douglas to Laxey which would have justified its location). The Act of Tynwald that permitted the building of the new church also ordered the demolition of the old one. No one got round to knocking down the old building. After several decades of abandonment it was 'discovered' by John Quine, the vicar of Lonan at the time, who set about restoring it.

In the graveyard, a few yards from the archway, there is a Celtic cross known as the Lonan Wheelcross which some have dated to the 5th century, it is standing in its original socket stone. At the far end of the churchyard is a shelter housing further crosses.

Marine Drive

Description: dramatic cliff top views, follows course of former railway: easy, 1½ -2½ miles.
OS map reference: 382742
From Douglas South Quay take the steep road up to Douglas Head (B80) underneath the archway to the Pigeon Stream car park.

Originally Marine Drive was built as a road from Douglas Head to Walberry in 1891 and extended to Whing a couple of years later. This was operated by Douglas Head Marine Drive Limited. The castellated entrance archway was the tollbooth – two large arches for horse drawn traffic, the smaller seaward arch for pedestrians. In 1896 it was decided to have a standard gauge tramway along the route: this was operated by the Douglas Southern Electric Tramway. It ran between Douglas Head as far as the beach resort of Port Soderick. The route ran atop the cliffs and crossed a number of spectacular viaducts and bridges. Pigeon Stream car park was the site of the equipment used to generate power for the tramway – the stream provided the water that was needed. The tramway ceased running in 1939.

Turn left up the gentle hill and notice the sheer cliffs that drop into the sea – this area has arguably some of the most dramatic coastal scenery on the Island. In stormy weather the waves can crash so furiously on the rocks far below that salty foam bubbles rise to land on the road. In the spring and summer the cliffs are home to hundreds of nesting seabirds (in particular gulls and choughs) and in unison their cries can be very noisy. As you leave the car park, in the near distance the pointed rock by the sea is known as the *'Nun's Chair'* – the area inland here used to be owned by the Nunnery which was located just south of Douglas.

On the inland side Douglas Head is home to herds of grazing sheep as well as the occasional off-road motorbike. Notice the folded, occasionally almost vertical, strata of the rocks. These sedimentary slate rocks were laid down about 480 million years ago when what is now the Isle of Man was located near the South Pole. They were originally in horizontal layers before the shifting and colliding of tectonic plates, of the old continents of Avalonia and Laurentia, caused the layers to

buckle into their current alignment. These rocks are the oldest visible parts of the Isle of Man so make sure you pause to touch them.

As you round the headland you now have a view of the coastline stretching to Langness and Castletown about 7 miles away. Beyond the gate across the road there is another mile of Marine Drive that can be walked, with the added benefit that there will be no motor vehicles on this stretch. This section has been closed to vehicular traffic since the 1960s due to the threat of rockfalls.

As you round the bend at Port Walberry you see a low wall which signifies where a bridge was built to take the tramway across the ravine. On the right at the bottom of the sheer cliff face you see sections where masonry has been installed to secure it after it was blasted away to allow the track to continue. And on the seaward side there are examples of similar work. This was an impressive feat of construction. Round the next bend you see a gully interestingly named Horseleap. Following another bend you see a large flat area on the seaward side called Little Ness. Being the largest level site on Marine Drive this spot was used as a depot for the trams. Paths cross it taking you towards the cliff edge and 180 degree panorama of the coast: you can see that the cliffs to the south are more subdued than those to the north. This is designated as a Dark Sky Discovery Site.

You have reached a second gate beyond which vehicular traffic resumes, so this is a good place to turn round and appreciate the dramatic cliff scenery from a different perspective as you walk back.

Maughold Church and Head

Description: historic church, carved Viking stones, walk in tranquil setting to lighthouse: easy, ¾ mile
OS map reference: 493917
Take A15 from Ramsey, there is a car park in the village.

Maughold has been an important Christian site from at least 7th century when a monastery was established by monks from Cumbria. The church has features that date from 11th and 12th centuries and the churchyard contains keeills and Celtic crosses from even earlier. The church is dedicated to St Maughold who is believed to have crossed the sea from Ireland and was cast ashore near the headland.

Enter the churchyard by the main gate and take the left path (clockwise) round the perimeter. Many of the gravestones are at least two centuries old. The path turns 90 degrees right and then takes a more gentle turn. Pause here and walk a few yards in the direction of the church.

You will soon see one of the three well-preserved keeills (early chapels) that are in the churchyard – this one is known as North Keeill. Maughold was an important early Christian site on the Island and has more keeills close to each other than any other place on the Island – the church itself is developed from a keeill. These small rectangular buildings, constructed from stone, were used by priests as places of solitary prayer and contemplation. The altar would be at the eastern end facing the Holy Land. From the door at the western end the priest would preach to members of the local community who had made the trip from their farms. If you walk further towards the church you will see the Middle Keeill.

Just beyond this is the grand grave of Captain Hugh Crow who was renowned as a more 'humane' slave trader. During the early 1800s there was a bounty of £100 paid to every captain if his 'passengers' were landed in good physical condition without any losses on the voyage – Crow achieved this regularly. It is alleged that he jumped into shark-infested waters to save a slave from drowning.

Return to the path and follow it to the gate that leads on to Maughold Head. On your right is the War Memorial and just beyond it is the Hall Caine Monument. Manx-born, Hall Caine originally was a teacher in the village but went on to become a prolific writer who outsold his contemporaries in Britain during the early part of 20th century. The East Keeill is nearby which has the churchyard well built into one of its corners – this was possibly the water supply for the monastery.

Continue round the path until you are level with the rear of the church: walk towards it and you will see the unprepossessing headstone of Edward Christian (died in 1660) who was one of the men who handed over the Island to Cromwell during the Civil War.

On the left of the path is an open building which houses a large

collection of crosses dating from 7th century. These are both Celtic Christian from 7th century and Norse following the Viking invasion and settlement of the Island from early 9th century. There is an information board on the right of the shelter and each cross has a reference number at its base.

Inside the church there are several noteworthy features, with the parish cross on the right being the most remarkable. The cross was made in the 14th century out of sandstone from St Bee's in Cumbria: it stood originally in the churchyard and, perhaps, looks a little out of place here. Among the various heraldic carvings there is one of the earliest known representations of the Three Legs of Man. One of the stained glass windows depicts Roolwer, the first Bishop of the Island. The interior was restored in 1900 in a style which does not echo the long history of this building.

Leave the churchyard by the gate at the east end and follow the track that heads gently uphill. Fifteen centuries ago a monastery was established here on Maughold Head – legend has it was situated by a never-failing spring. If you go left to the small grassed carpark there is a kissing gate on the right which leads to a steep, occasionally slippery, path down to Chibbyr Vaghal, St Maughold's Well, the location of this spring. Legend has it that St Maughold, who was the Island's first bishop, was originally a ne'er do well living in Ireland. However, he was converted by St Patrick and begged to atone for his past misdeeds. For this he was cast adrift in a small boat which eventually landed here: the spring is supposed to mark where he scrambled ashore and thanked the Lord for his survivial.

If you proceed straight ahead along the track you will soon come to Maughold Lighthouse (built in 1914) which is the most easterly point on the Island and closest to England – St Bee's is about 30 miles distant. There are over 100 steps down to the lighthouse but a gate prevents access to the bottom. Nearby are private dwellings which used to be lighthouse keepers' cottages.

Meayll Circle, Cregneash

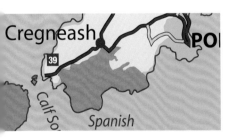

Description: well-preserved 5,000 year old ceremonial site with views over to the Calf of Man: easy, ½ mile
OS map reference: 189679
Take A31 to Cregneash, immediately after leaving village turn right up a minor road and park just when you see tracks leading uphill on the right.

Follow the track, bear left and pass a series of low concrete and brick buildings which must be military look-outs judging by the narrow slits in the walls. Meayll Hill has impressive views of the Calf of Man on your left and Gansey Bay on the right and Port Erin directly in front.

The path sweeps down to the left across the heather and gorse.

The site itself is in a hollow although it does have a good views downslope to the north, and it can be seen for a mile in that direction. The site was doubtless chosen due to its dominant position – commanding awe and respect of the nearby communities. In Manx Gaelic it is called *Lhiaght ny Virragh* which translates as 'cairn of the pointed rock'.

Meayll Circle stands near to the summit of Meayll Hill (Mull Hill) and provides evidence of occupation from Neolithic to Medieval times. This impressive Neolithic grave and ceremonial site dates back to around 3500 BC. This pre-dates Stonehenge which was probably built around 2,500BC.

There are six burial chambers laid out in a circle with gaps between them. Each has a short passage formed by standing stones with a pair of burial chambers at right angles to the left and right (12 in total). Three of them are more intact and give a good impression of what the overall site may have looked like originally. It is likely that the chambers would have been covered by rocks, earth and grass, so one would have had to crawl to gain access to the chambers. A white rock is embedded in the ground in centre of the circle: this would have glinted in the sun and have attracted the attention of the people in the settlements nearby.

When the site was excavated in 1893 and 1911 fragments of urns were found. It is probable that these urns were used to hold the remains of the dead and several were placed in each burial chamber. Shards of ornate pottery, charred bones, flint tools and white quartz pebbles have all been found in the burial chambers and can be viewed at the Manx Museum.

On a hill opposite is a navigational aid for international aircraft which looks rather like the typical shape of a UFO!

Millennium Oakwood

Description: stroll round commemorative wood in a picturesque setting, sword of state monument; easy, 1 mile
OS map reference: 365779
Take Peel Road out of Douglas, at Braddan Oak Tree head uphill towards New Nobles Hospital: just before hospital there is a sports ground car park on the right. Walk back to the road and turn right with the hospital on your left. In a couple of hundred yards there is a gate on the right leading into the Oakwood.

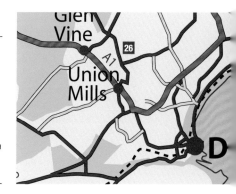

On 9th March 2000 every primary school child on the Island planted an oak sapling to create the Millennium Oakwood. Eighteen months previously acorns had been distributed throughout the primary schools

so that every child could grow their own sapling. On the day over 6,500 children were transported by bus and rail from their schools to plant their contribution – regular bus services had to be cancelled for the day. At the bottom of the wood the information board tells the location of each school's trees.

The children's programme Blue Peter broadcast the opening. A song was specially written for the day, the chorus was

I planted an acorn
I hoped it would grow, as it should, as it should
I'm planting an oak tree
To make a Millennium Wood

The woodland is an oasis of peace on the edge of Douglas, it used by dog walkers and hospital workers out for a stroll. There are several paths that take one round the plantation. As you wander marvel at how some oaks have grown to be over 20 feet high with massive spreading branches while others nearby are small. Occasionally this may be down to the different genetics of the original acorns or the way that different pupils planted the saplings in the first place. But often this has arisen because original saplings that have failed to grow properly have been replaced by new plants (mainly since 2010) so the trees are not of equivalent age. It is heartening to see that the 25 trees planted by special needs pupils (plot 18 by the lower entrance) are the original saplings and all look to have flourished.

In the centre is the Millennium Monument with an enlarged Sword of State passing through a globe representing the solar system. This is placed on a replica of Tynwald Hill: notice the four tiers the lowest of which sports the Three Legs of Man. Apparently, the structure acts as a sundial. From here there are great views across Douglas to the east and of the Mountain Road to the north, with the white building high up being the TT landmark of Kate's Cottage.

National Park and Arboretum

Description: extensive park and woodland in beautiful setting: easy ½ – 1½ miles
OS map reference: 279818
The Douglas to Peel road (A1) runs through St John's, there is a car park signed National Arboretum close to Tynwald Hill.

The park was created in 1979 to mark the millennium anniversary of Tynwald – the world's longest running continuous parliament and is near to Tynwald Hill where the parliament meets once a year. It is set in 25 acres of gently sloping countryside.

As you go through the gabled wooden gate you will quite quickly come across a large number of ducks of various species that live in the pond. Often they are lurking on the paths waiting for visitors to feed them.

The park comprises two main sections. The section that is closer to the entrance and the pond is crossed by concrete or wooden paths and grassed rides. It comprises a wide range of less common largely ornamental trees and shrubs. They are grouped in areas each of which bears the name of one of the Island's 17 parishes. There are no set routes so just wander where the fancy takes you or, if you are more organised, adopt a clockwise or anti-clockwise loop. There is a children's nature trail featuring characters from the Gruffalo.

There is a memorial erected by the Burma Star Association in the eastern part which is flanked by two stands of bamboo. To the left is a tree planted by US astronaut Nicole Stott who photographed a unique view of the Isle of Man during her voyage on the space shuttle Discovery in 2011. Her connection to the Island is through her Manx-born husband

space ambassador Chris Stott. Across the whole park the tree plaques and benches commemorate a range of significant dignitaries and national events. Beyond this is a children's playground.

The second section can be explored by heading towards the higher ground where there are no formal paths. This area to the north and east accommodates hardier, mainly native tree species. Around the trees you will see wild flowers, like the purple foxglove, and blackcurrant brambles. At the top of the main hill is a three-sided shelter. From here there is a panoramic view extending south over St John's Church and village, and towering above is the tree clad Slieau Whallian. Legend has it that Slieau Whallian was the site, centuries ago, of punishments that were meted out to those accused of witchcraft. As a test of their innocence or guilt the unfortunate person was put into a barrel, with sharp iron spikes pointing inwards. The barrel was rolled down the slope. It was deemed that only those guilty of witchcraft could survive this ordeal. They would subsequently be put to death – perhaps by drowning in the river at the foot of the hill. Those who died were deemed innocent – an early example of a Catch 22 situation.

Further uphill there is a trail through pine trees.

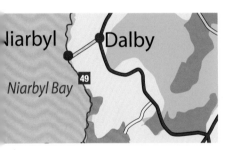

Niarbyl Bay

Description: picturesque bay and clifftop walk, chance to straddle two continents: easy, 1 mile
OS map reference: 212777
Take A27 from Peel, at Dalby turn right down minor road signed Niarbyl. There is a car park at the café and Visitor Centre. There are information boards and a telescope behind the building.

Leave the car park for a short walk down the road to Niarbyl Bay. Niarbyl is Manx for *tail* on account of the series of rocks stretching out into the sea. This is arguably one of the most picturesque small bays on the Island with stunning views south of the cliffs culminating in those of the Calf of Man. The thatched fisherman's cottage on the right has been used in several films. The famous music hall artiste Florrie Forde of the early 20th century had a summer cottage in Niarbyl, which she used when she was performing in Douglas.

If you walk down the jetty past the cottage you can visit a most momentous site. Walk across the pebbly beach and you will see a narrow band of white rock in the cliff. This marks the area where two ancient continental land masses collided over 140 million years ago. The south is the grey slate (Manx Group) of the continent of Gondwana from which southern England and Africa were formed. To the north the rocks are sandstone (Dalby Group) which were on the continent known as

Laurentia of which Scotland and North America are parts. Originally these two continents were separated by Iapetus Ocean which was several thousand miles wide. Slowly the tectonic plates moved (continental drift) and the Iapetus Ocean was completely closed at the point that you are looking at (Iapetus Suture fault line). At low tide you can place your feet either side of the white band and be standing on two continents simultaneously!

As the lobster pots on the sea wall testify, Niarbyl is still used as a fishing harbour – at its peak 20 or more fishing boats would be moored here. Just behind the bungalow on the left there is a path which takes you round the headland – signed Niarbyl Coastal Footpath. The path is a gentle climb, in places there are wooden foot boards with handrails to ease the journey. The view back is of the tail rocks colonised by seabirds and the crystal clear waters of the bay. At one point there is a narrow gap between two cliff faces which would make an interesting photograph. The path cuts through gorse hedges with their distinctive smell which some liken to coconut.

The path then bends sharp left. From here one can descend, relatively steeply, to the bay. Alternatively, one can admire the view and turn back. On returning to the harbour there is a short path in front of the bungalow which leads to a small thatched cottage (Knockuskey). At the time of writing the path beyond was closed.

Onchan
Douglas Bay

Onchan Wetlands

Description: small but perfectly formed and peaceful nature reserve in centre of old Onchan village: easy, ¼ mile.

OS map reference: 400782

Take the Douglas to Laxey Road (A2), after the traffic lights in Onchan take the third right turn heading down towards the church. There is kerb-side parking before or by the church.

Church Road is known as *The Butt* – derived from the barrels or butts that were used to store water before the advent of sanitised mains supply. The sign on the wall on the left side of Church Road says *Onchan Village Green*, walk through to the end where there is an information board for Onchan Wetlands Nature Reserve. Here you will learn that this was originally the site of a dam for a mill which was last used in the 1930s. The area silted up and in the 1990s volunteers worked to reinstate the pond and build a short circular boardwalk. The area is referred to as a curragh, the term for marshy, boggy land – the largest example of which is in the north of the Island near Ballaugh.

Follow the elevated wooden walkway through the resplendent wet woodland vegetation with willow being the main tree species. This small area is typical of how large areas of the Island might have looked about 15,000 years ago as the last ice caps melted creating extensive marshy land which began to be colonised by plants and trees. If you come in the early spring clouds of frogspawn can be seen in the pools of water.

As you return to the entrance turn left and cross the road. The wall that surrounds St. Peter's Churchyard was built to include a large wedge-shaped stone (near the lamp post). It is alleged that children were warned that it was a whipping post and that if they misbehaved that they'd be taken there for punishment. In reality, it is most likely all that remains of a semi-circle of stones of an ancient burial site.

The origins of the church on this site date back to 12th and 13th centuries; however, the present one was completed in 1833. The oldest gravestone in the churchyard is that of John Cannell who died in 1641. Onchan derived its name from the patron saint of the parish St Christopher who was known by his Manx Gaelic name of *Conchenn*.

Peel Headland

Description: glorious views of Peel Castle and surrounding countryside, a look back into the town's interesting past: easy 1¼ miles
OS map reference: 250842
Drive to the extreme north end of the Prom (Marine Parade) where there is plenty of parking. This area and up to the headland is known as *Creg Malin* which translates from Manx as 'Rock of the hill brow'.

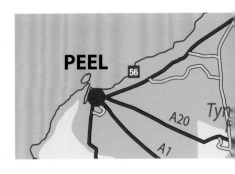

With the decline of herring fishing in late 19th century Peel embraced the burgeoning visitor industry with the building of the Promenade (begun in 1886) and a number of grand boarding houses. Most have been turned into flats. However, before this these buildings and those up the hill immediately behind were used as an internment camp during World War 2 for citizens of enemy countries who were living in Britain, but were deemed potentially a risk to be at liberty. Barbed wire, manned by soldiers, enclosed the area around these buildings: the views of the bay and the castle must have been some compensation for their confinement.

Walk along the pavement past a bowling club and café and the tennis courts and BMX track. Take a flight of concrete steps towards what looks like a green bus shelter which is pretty unique. Unfortunately it no longer works, but by day it did function as a FM/DAB radio and at night a press of the button provided one hour of light. Follow the tarmac path as it leads uphill towards the gorse. Don't take the first concrete path on the right, but head up to the top of the hill where there is a Millennium Cross and an information board. The cliffs are made of red sandstone which occurs only in a relatively small area around Peel. These rocks were formed about 380 million years ago in desert conditions

when what is now the Isle of Man was located near the Equator. The stone has been quarried for the construction of many buildings locally – the oldest of which is the 10th century round tower on St Patrick's Isle (Peel Castle).

This is a great place to take in the panorama of the city (it is considered so as it has a cathedral) and castle of Peel and the series of hill summits that culminates with Corrin's Tower, or Corrin's Folly as it is known locally. The view of the coast on the right stretches as far as Jurby whose white church can be seen in the distance over 10 miles away.

Continue on the lower level path as it curves right, take the path on the right that crosses the grass. This leads to a walkway and a flight of steps to the site of the open air baths known as Traie Fogog (translates as misty shore). They were opened in 1896 and originally called the Empress Baths in honour of Queen Victoria's diamond jubilee: at that time they were the largest of their kind in Europe. The opening was marked by a demonstration of *'a number of difficult and novel feats'* – the Victorian equivalent of synchronised swimming. At first the changing rooms were tents on the beach. In 1923 new owners took over and built the platforms and had changing rooms installed – the concrete remains of which you can see. The baths were popular and operated until the 1950s.

Return to the main path by the blue Coastal Footpath sign and follow the path past several benches which are a testimony to how popular this walk is with the locals. Pass a pair of gateposts which are all that is left to mark the site of a guest house run by the Cooperative Holiday Association that stood here from 1913 to the 1960s. The path narrows with a fence on the right which suggests that one is close to, but safe from, the cliff edge. The path curves right and there is a bench inscribed with *'Traa Dy* Liooar' (translates as time enough) – this a great place to pause to admire the views before returning the way that you came.

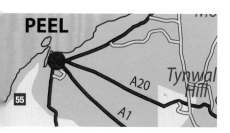

Peel Hill and Corrin's Tower

Description: hill walk with impressive views of Peel's Castle and harbour, 19th century folly: easy to moderate, 1½ miles.
OS map reference: 246682
There is plenty of parking near Peel Castle or at Fenella Beach.

The start of the path is marked by a tall carving of Fenella standing at the foot of the rocks by the car park: it is named after the character in Sir Walter Scott's Peveril of the Peak. There is an excellent information board which describes all that you will encounter. Walk to the left of the statue up the steps which soon give way to a concrete path. As you

climb you begin to look down on the attractive harbour and town: the only detraction being the incinerator tower. There are several benches where one can rest and take in the views.

Crossing over a concrete road the path now is on grassland for the remainder of the walk. Cross over another track heading towards a bench on the immediate skyline. The panorama now opens up to include the hills in the centre of the Island and you should be able to spot Snaefell with twin radio masts on its peak. At 2,036 feet Snaefell qualifies as being the Island's only mountain. Beyond this point the gradients are gentler, but if you are only out for a short stroll this could be a good point to head back.

Immediately below Peel Castle is laid out for you. The site, St Patrick's Isle, was originally separated from Peel at high tide but a narrow causeway would appear at low tide to allow access. Evidence suggests that the site was inhabited permanently from about 1000BC – its location cut off from the rest of the land would help those who lived there feel safe. About 500AD it was settled by early Christians (coming over from Ireland) who built a chapel. Although it is named after St Patrick it is unlikely that the saint would have visited there.

Following the Viking conquest, Magnus Barelegs built a fortified hall

in 11th century and the castle grew bit by bit for the next 200 years. The oldest part is actually the round tower which dates from the tenth century. Secular and religious interests grew alongside each other: the now ruined cathedral (to the right of the site) was built in 13th century by Bishop Simon. The curtain wall around the Isle was built in the middle of 15th century by Thomas Stanley, the First Earl of Derby and ruler of Isle of Man, to further fortify the castle. The castle is home to the supernatural *Moddey Dhoo*, a large black dog which haunts the passages – the supposed first siting and the start of the legend dates to the 1660s.

During the 1980s the site was studied extensively and many artefacts were unearthed. The most significant find was the grave of a noble Viking woman complete with a variety of jewellery (on display in Manx Museum).

It is short tug uphill to the crag and you begin to have good views of Corrin's Tower at the top of the hill. From here the track across the heather, gorse and bracken is clearly visible. The next stretch is on the flat, then downhill and a gentle ascent to the gate in the stone wall. Judging by the tower on the left the mobile phone reception should be excellent. The path rises and falls as you head towards the Tower. To the left is a white triangulation pillar: usually the Ordnance Survey locate these at the highest point but the Tower had been built there first!

The main tower is encircled by six smaller ones. Corrin's Tower, or Corrin's Folly as it is known locally, is 50 feet high and built around 1806 by Mr Thomas Corrin in memory of his wife Alice who had died in childbirth. He farmed at Knockaloe Beg in the valley nearby. To the side is a rectangular low walled area where he is buried with his wife and his two children. Originally his son Robert, who was a devout Anglican, had Thomas buried in consecrated ground in Kirk Patrick churchyard. However, one night his father's friends moved his body to a hiding place and it was later buried by the Tower! Fearing that his son might not respect the Tower Thomas had it entrusted to Trinity House who used it for coastguard duties until the 1920s – they looked after the site in return.

To the south the grassed farmland is known as Knockaloe. This was the site of an internment camp for enemy aliens (mainly Germans and Austrians) during the First World War. It housed about 25,000 internees making it the largest such camp in the world. Nothing remains of the camp as they were mainly wooden huts designed to be temporary structures only. Other traces were erased soon after the war as there was some collective embarrassment about imprisoning civilians many of whom had lived in Britain for years and showed no enemy sympathies.

Return by the route that you came by. On a clear day over to the west (your left) you might see the outline of the Mountains of Mourne in Northern Ireland. On the way down don't be misled by the curving concrete track, take the smaller path straight ahead. You can reward yourself at the end of the walk by having a Manx Kipper Bap from the café on the breakwater.

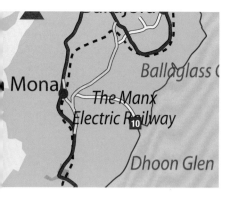

Port Cornaa

Description: beach, river and woodland walk, with an opportunity to paddle in salt and fresh water; easy, ¾ mile.

OS Map Reference: 473879

Take A2 Laxey to Ramsey coast road, after Laxey and just beyond Dhoon take a right turn on to a minor road which immediately crosses the railway line. After a few hundred yards take right turn down minor road heading for Port Cornaa – this itself is a beautiful drive. There is parking at the end of the road at the edge of the beach.

Start by walking to the water's edge across the beach. This is formed of storm-tossed pebbles and rocks and so is constantly shifting its shape. It is gradually growing in height as the storm tides lift stones off the bottom and hurl them up the beach. The enormous size of the pebbles is a tribute to the power of the waves. The small building on your right (looking out to sea) used to house telecommunications equipment and was the place where the cable from England arrived on the Isle of Man.

Return inland and follow the green footpath sign heading towards the footbridge that crosses the river. At high tide this flat area becomes a salt lagoon and the path can become flooded briefly. Bluebells, montbretias and ferns populate the area. Cross over a second bridge and continue along the path through the woodland where, in late spring, you will have the heady smell of wild garlic. Continue past the footpath sign, the bank here is covered in flowers of many different colours in early summer.

On the left are the incomplete buildings of what was intended to be an ammunition factory. In 1885 a Swedish chemist, Carl Lamm, invented Bellite, a new form of explosive which was impossible to activate without a specific detonator. This made it much safer than dynamite that could easily explode by impact, misuse or extreme heat. Lamm wanted to manufacture his new product in the UK but there were very strict regulations in place regarding this. No such rules on the production of explosives currently applied on the Isle of Man so in 1890

he commenced the construction of his factory in this remote location. However, the Manx Government began to have concerns. They sought advice from the UK who recommended that the same safety regulations should be applied on the Island. These would make Lamm's production process uneconomic, so he never completed the factory. Notice how a large tree is growing through the walls as nature reclaims the area.

The path climbs marginally uphill and, immediately after the gate, hairpin left down towards the river. It widens out into a large flat area that is well-suited to picnicking, The river here is often used for paddling in the summer: there is a small waterfall nearby.

You can return back to the main path to extend your walk in the woodland or turn tight through the gate to return to the car park.

Port e Vullen

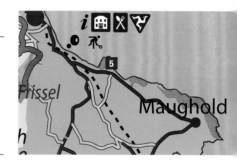

Description: walk along low cliffs and beach, stroll through picturesque hamlet with unique phone box: easy
1 mile
OS Map Reference: 470929
Leave Ramsey heading south on A2 and soon bear left on to A15 (signed Port Lewaigue). Cross the railway line and at the blue sign for the Coastal Footpath take the narrow road to the left where there is a small car park.

This can only be walked at low tide
There are two information boards by the car park. These describe in detail the views in front of you and the history of the area. Port Lewaigue was used as a harbour in 18th and 19th centuries to land limestone from Castletown and ship out iron that was mined at Maughold.

Leave the car park by a grass path heading to the low sea wall with views northwards of The Queen's Pier and the sandy cliffs of Ramsey Bay leading to the Point of Ayre. As the sea wall finishes, the path goes gently uphill to skirt round the shallow cliffs: following rain this section can be a little muddy. This headland has the wonderful Manx name of *Gob ny rona* which translates as 'division point' or 'seal point'.

Short raised walkways with handrails take one over the places where small brooks trickle towards the sea. Across one inlet is a derelict concrete structure which is a former bathing creek. Pink, white and blue flowers line the path in spring, with reddy orange montbretias taking over in the summer. As you go round views of Maughold Brooghs open up in front of you.

A flight of concrete steps takes you down through a gap in the slate cliff onto the shingle and sand beach. This is known as Port e Vullen which has an old spelling of *Port ny Mwyllin* meaning 'harbour of the mill'. There is a delightful little waterfall running tumbling down a gap in the rocks – the mill, no longer there, would have been situated upstream. Jump over the stream and take a sharp right up the concrete slipway to the main road where one turns left uphill.

On reaching the road, turn right on the road through Port Lewaigue – the Manx for 'harbour by the sloping creek'. On the left there is a disused red telephone box which has been converted into a book exchange library – known as Maughold Exchange. Proceed through the hamlet and turn right back down to the car park.

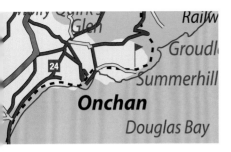

Port Jack Glen

Description: peaceful and attractive park, walk by stream: easy, ½ mile
OS map reference: 399773
Follow Douglas Prom north, as you climb the hill turn left immediately after Port Jack chippy and park safely nearby. The lower entrance to the glen is just behind the row of shops on the corner.

Until Onchan Commissioners took control in 1959 the area was simply an undeveloped and overgrown valley at the foot of Royal Avenue. Subsequently it has been landscaped with paths, bridges and steps with plantings of bushes and flowering plants. The stream has been dug out to form to small ponds. There is a circular path to the top of the glen, where this is a shelter, and back down.

As you sit on one of the benches notice the houses on both sides of the glen. These formed Onchan internment camp, holding German and Austrian alien civilians during World War 2. The surrounding streets were fenced with barbed wire. The camp ran from June 1940 to July 1941, and was re-opened in October 1941 to house mainly Italian internees until November 1944.

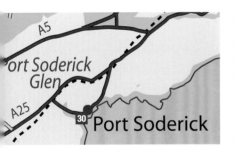

Port Soderick

Description: woodland walk by rushing stream, secluded scenic bay: easy, ½ mile.
OS map reference: 346726
Take the Old Castletown Road (A25) from Douglas, turn left down a minor road (B23) signposted Port Soderick. At the end of the road there is parking by the entrance to the glen.

The path through woodland populated with spring flowers follows the course of the Crogga River. The river enters the sea at a scenic bay.

This is a delightful glen, in particular in spring and early summer when the daffodils, bluebells and wild garlic contribute their colours and scents to the walk. It was adopted by the Government as a Manx National Glen in 1975. On entering the glen take the right path, which is well maintained, keeping the Crogga River on your left. You pass open areas which are often used for picnics. This area can become a little boggy: in the past cars that parked here would occasionally become trapped and the local farmer would pull out with his tractor for a fee of £25!

Towards the end the path rises gently to wooden fencing, here one can take a brief diversion by following the steps uphill on the right. The path curves right and flattens giving you views of the glen from high up. This path eventually takes you out of the glen, so walk a few hundred yards further to appreciate the view before heading back.

Re-join the main path and head downstream. Cross the bridge so now the river is on your left. The path climbs a little way into the woodland before dropping down to the riverbank. Follow this path pass the main bridge and ascend a short flight of stone steps. Pass through the gate and follow the concrete track to the bay.

Port Soderick was a thriving destination for holidaymakers in late 19th and early 20th centuries. The name Port Soderick very appropriately translates from the Norse as *sunny* or *south-facing creek*. It offered refreshment rooms, side show stalls, an amusement arcade and boating: candles were sold to explore the caves (to the right as you look out to the sea). The large building on the right formerly housed an amusement arcade and paddling pool. There was a cliff top tramway from Douglas Head which transported visitors in their hundreds each day during the summer. To reach the beach there was a funicular railway which ran down the cliff to the bottom. On the pillar by a flight of steps leading to the breakwater one can see a plaque which references the Forrester brothers, the entrepreneurs who established these facilities in 1897.

The site is now sadly derelict: the last attraction being a restaurant owned by the celebrity chef Kevin Woodford. However, at the time of writing Heritage Great Britain, which owns tourist sites at Land's End and John o Groats, has recently purchased the land with a view to revitalising it as a leisure destination.

The Raggatt

Description: woodland and riverside walk, where loved ones are remembered: easy, ½ mile
OS map reference: 242829
On the A27 from Peel to Patrick park at the lay-by on the left as the road bends right.

The name is probably derived from the Scandinavian *Rargata* which translates as 'roe path or track' – roe being a female deer. Follow the path through the gate as it bends left, over the river, into the park. The bridge on the left over the Neb leads into a more rugged woodland, whereas the main area is more formally laid out. Each memorial tree is numbered and there is an occasional plaque. Along the path if you bear left up the grassy bank you reach the river's edge. The path proceeds further upstream, you can bear left to walk through gorse-lined path

which is very fragrant when it is in bloom.

This path continues into the countryside along the river for another mile with views of open farmland opening up on the right. Alternatively, to head back to the wooded area turn right when you meet the main path again. Just at the back bridge back over the stream take a grassed path on the left to complete a short loop back to the entrance around the edge of the trees.

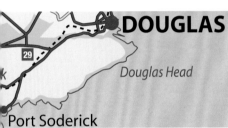

Real Fairy Bridge

Description: countryside walk to secret place of folklore interest: easy, 1 mile.
OS map reference: 357748
Take the A6 from south Douglas, after going under the railway bridge Kewaigue School car park on the right is a convenient start point.

The Fairy Bridge best known to tourists is that on the A5 road from Douglas to Castletown in Santon by Ballona Bridge. However, the 'Real Fairy Bridge' as it is known to locals, and shown as the 'Fairy Bridge' on old Ordnance Survey maps, is located in Kewaigue in the southern outskirts of Douglas.

Turn right out of the car park and walk uphill along the pavement. After 100 yards cross over the road through the gateway which has a red bin by it. Follow the track ahead keeping the farm buildings on your left. The path can be a little muddy after heavy rain. On the left is sheep pasture leading up to Douglas Head. The track slopes downhill towards a stream.

Just before the stream the take the path on the right along the bank. After a few yards you will come to a derelict and overgrown bridge – the Fairy Bridge itself. In the wall people leave small gifts to the 'little people' to encourage them to grant them their wish. For instance, it is customary to leave a coin to please them so that they do not cause mishaps to happen to you in the year to come. The path continues briefly on the other side of the bridge (look out for the old tree stump where gifts are also placed) but soon becomes too overgrown to progress further. The riverbank is crowded with beautiful flowers in spring.

To past generations of Manx people fairies are very different beings

from those written about in Britain. From Peter Pan we have an image of Tinkerbell who is only a few inches high and has gossamer wings. To the Manx fairies are three or four feet high with an appearance more like a Hobbit, and definitely no wings. A good Manxman, however, does not call them fairies – the word *ferish*, a corruption of the English, did not exist on the Island one hundred and fifty years ago. Instead, it was customary (and still is) to refer to them as 'themselves', 'the little people' or *Mooinjer Veggey* (in Manx) rather than fairies. They live in communities and enjoy hunting and feasting and music-making. Fairies have a range of abilities – strength, skill, invisibility, shape-shifting; they can bring good luck or bad luck to a person or household depending on how one deals with them. Thus, one should always greet them as you drive past the popularly-adopted Fairy Bridge on the Castletown Road.

Return to the car park by the same route.

Scarlett Point

Description: varied coastline walk with several places of special note, remains of limestone quarrying: easy, 1 mile
OS map reference: 258666
Follow the road into Castletown passing Castle Rushen and the main square on the right. Leave the Square following a brown sign indicating Scarlett Visitors Centre and take the first left down Queen Street passing rows of cottages on either side. Follow the road until it ends by the sea shore where there is a car park.

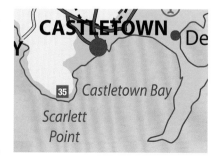

Scarlett is situated on the coastal footpath, it's name is derived from the Norse *Skarfakluft* meaning cormorant's ledge.

The limestone rocks in the area were formed around 330 million years ago when the landform that was to become the Isle of Man had drifted northwards to reach the equator. At that time the land was covered by warm seas in which millions of small sea creatures lived. When these died they fell to the bottom and their shells, which were composed of calcium carbonate, formed the carboniferous limestone found around Castletown. On the right is a flooded quarry from which large quantities of limestone was extracted from the 1870s to build Castletown station and the bridges of the Steam Railway: it was worked until 1930. A pair of swans or a flock of ducks are usually in residence here, and in summer large lily pads spread over the water's surface adding charm to the former industrial site.

The Visitor Centre (open Friday – Sunday from 2 – 5pm from May to early September plus Bank Holidays) was formerly the quarry manager's office. Every few hundred yards you will notice a number painted on the wall – these denote eight locations of interest to investigate off the path (guide available in Visitor's Centre).

Some of the more notable features include:

1. The top of the three limekilns on the way up from the car park on the left. Initially, small quarries were opened on the seaward side of the Visitor Centre. The kilns were used to heat limestone to high temperatures to convert it to quicklime: slaked lime (calcium hydroxide) would be formed by mixing it with water, this would be used as a fertiliser on farmland.

2. The undulating limestone in the foreground owes its appearance to quarrying. The small stone building was probably a tool shed for the quarrymen. The large dome shaped rock rising out of the

sea in the background is the Stack which is an old volcanic vent now plugged with basalt.

3. This basalt-filled dyke running seawards through the limestone platform was opened up by shifting continental plates following the Carboniferous era (about 300 million years ago).

6. A number of rock pools with different levels of salinity – some are brackish and others filled with fresh clean water. Different plants grow in pools depending on the amount of salt in the water. The carpet of purple (milk vetch), blue (spring quill), white (sea campion) and pink (thrift) flowers is at its best during spring and early summer.

8. A panoramic view of the island extending from the Chicken Rock Lighthouse in the south to Snaefell with its two aerials in the north. The derelict buildings are all that remain of RAF Scarlett (World War II) which included a top secret radar station known as 'Chain Home'.

Retrace your steps to the car park.

Silverdale Glen

Description: woodland walk by babbling stream feeding in to duck pond, historic merry-go-round: additional river walk past historic pack-horse bridge: easy, 1-2¼ miles
OS map reference: 275710
At Ballasalla roundabout (on A5, Castletown Road) head north signed A26 St Marks and Foxdale. Straight over the next roundabout and in a few hundred yards take a left turn and another left turn signed Silverdale. Just over a small bridge there is a car park by the Silverdale Glen café. If this is busy follow signs to additional car park but return to this one to start the walk.

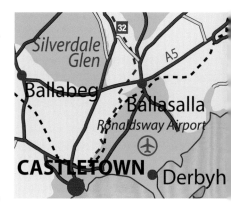

The site includes a pottery shop and boating lake together with a children's playground including a magnificent Victorian water powered roundabout and a large grassed area which allows space for games and picnicking. It was established as a recreational area in the late 19th century. The Cregg Mill by the bridge was built in about 1767 to process flax: it is now the home of Manx Ices which are sold in the café. The boating lake was originally the dam providing water for the wheel in the mill.

There are two short walks from here.

The more popular walk is to take the path round the pond keeping it on your right. At the end of the pond is a white building which used to be the Silverburn Glen Mineral Water factory. Ignore the uphill path on the left which takes one to a car park, instead carry on forwards.

Follow the path with the Silverburn River on your left, pass the bridge on the right which you can take on the way back. Over the small metal bridge where the river bifurcates, with the small stream going through the sluice gate. The path narrows a little as you head upstream and ends at the main road.

Return by the same route and this time cross over the wooden bridge and right down the steps. In a few hundred yards there is a bridge which takes you across a grassy picnic area to the playground. The roundabout was constructed in about 1890 and is the only surviving and working one in Europe, to be driven by water. In the 1980s the original horses started to deteriorate and replacements were made. If you look carefully you will notice that each one is different. If you scrutinise them in detail you will see that the outside of the outside horse is more decorative than the outside of the inside horse, and that the inside of the inside horse is more decorative than the inside of the outside horse. It requires a certain power of logic to reason why this should be the case.

Return to the car park and walk up the road for 20 yards until you reach a wooden fence by an information board on the left: this is the entrance to the second, lower glen walk. After a few yards take the path that hairpins left down towards the stream. You will see a plaque commemorating when the glen was given over by the Quine family to the Manx National Trust. Continue down the path through the woods favouring the slightly higher track. You will encounter a weir with a narrow channel.

Follow the higher path which has a couple of concrete steps. This slopes gently downhill where you will see the Monk's Well on the right – the monks being from nearby Rushen Abbey, but more about them later. The plaque encourages one to toss a small offering into the well while a prayer, vow or (in modern days) a wish is said. Continue and take a brief detour over the bridge to see the mill pond which is usually home to a family of ducks. Return to the path which passes through a pair of low gateposts, which have the words 'Silverdale Glen' and 'Grey Tower'

(the name of a large house on Silverdale Road) on them, and bear left.

You are now on the Millennium Way which is a 25 mile path that runs from Ramsey to Castletown: it was established to commemorate a thousand years of Tynwald, the Manx Parliament, in 1979. This route is shared by the Bayr ny Skeddan (translates as *'Way of the herring'*) which runs from Peel to Castletown. This is an old packhorse route used to transport fish caught in Peel across to the then capital in the south. However, it is very likely that the smell of the herrings was used to conceal the presence of contraband spirits that also made the journey!

On the right, obscured by bushes, there is the remains of what was probably a lime kiln. Kilns were used to heat limestone to high temperatures to convert it to quicklime: slaked lime (calcium hydroxide) would be formed by mixing it with water, this would be used as a fertiliser on farmland. Limestone was quarried at Scarlett, just south of Castletown, until the 1930s. The path ends with the pack-horse bridge in front of you, exit on to a narrow road via a wooden gate on your right. It is called the Monks' Bridge and is also known as *Crossag*, in Manx this means 'Little crossing'. The bridge was built in 1350 by the Cistercian monks of nearby Rushen Abbey which was established in 1134. The pack-horse bridge allowed the monks to pass over the Silverburn River to travel to their farms in the north, and also to give access to the Abbot's gallows which were situated about a mile north at Black Hill. It is believed to be the best preserved medieval bridge in the British Isles.

Continue along this road with the river on your left until it ends in a ford. In front of you is the Abbey Restaurant and on the left of the car park a path leads to the entrance of Rushen Abbey. Unless you have a couple of hours to spare to explore the Abbey this a good point to turn back. On the return you may want to take some of the paths that lead closer to the river, safe in the knowledge that they will return you to the main path eventually.

Snaefell

Description: The Island's only mountain (just) with immense panoramic views of the 7 Kingdoms: moderate to steep, 2 miles.
OS map reference: 389859
Take the Mountain Road (A18) to the Bungalow where there is parking.

At 2,036 feet Snaefell is the Island's only mountain – 2,000 feet being the recognised altitude for mountains in the British Isles. Due to its exposed position results it is usually covered by snow for many weeks in winter – earning the name Norse name *Snaefijal* or 'snow hill'. Although the path is well-used by family groups, this ascent is for the

more serious walker as there are a couple of short, steep sections. As Snaefell is somewhat a national treasure, the path is well maintained. And when you have walked it you will feel far more satisfied than those who just took the Mountain Railway. The railway from Laxey to the summit was built in a few months and opened in August 1895: all the passenger cars date from that year.

There is a well-defined track through grass, heather and peat cuttings which starts from a clearly signed kissing gate. Mid-way there is a short passage of slate paving which could be a little slippery if it has rained recently. There are beautiful views down the valley, which has been carved by glaciers, towards Laxey. For the last few hundred feet the path becomes less defined, it would be best to take the track on the right heading towards the left of the two radio masts.

On reaching the flat top walk in front of the Summit Hotel. The original wooden building was installed for the railway's opening in 1895: there were boarded walkways to different vantage points at the summit. Due to the railway's popularity a larger, replacement stone building with turrets was opened in 1902. A fire gutted the building in 1982 (which was allowed to burn out owing to the remote location and inaccessibility for the fire brigade) and the building was renovated completely. As there is no water supply at the summit each day a tram delivers a bowser of drinking water for use in the restaurant.

Follow the concrete path and handrail to reach the concrete trig point which marks the highest point. There is an information plaque indicating which directions to look to see the adjacent countries – it is possible to see over 60 miles. In fact, there is a saying that from Snaefell, on a clear day, one can see Seven Kingdoms – those of Mann, Scotland, Ireland, Wales, England, Neptune and Heaven.

In one of the most curious races Snaefell was the end point of an annual race from Blackpool Tower held in the 1970s. There were different classes of race depending on whether engine power was used for part or all of the route. The race was sponsored by Heineken and entrants were obliged to carry a can of their product which had to be consumed as the end.

From afar Snaefell is easily recognisable by its pair of radio masts. These form part of UK Air Traffic Control tracking system and are the first beacons whose radio transmissions are picked up by planes after they have crossed the Atlantic. They also provide transmission for Island facilities including mobile, internet and television. It is a pity that they are placed on such an elevated and scenic spot, but in the Victorian era the construction of the hotel and the mountain railway set the precedent of having man-made edifices on Snaefell

The descent is by the same route as ascent, or by train now that you have walked the hard part. To start the walk down head to final post of the electric railway and proceed left downhill, where you will soon pick up a proper path. Near the end of the descent you can bear left for 50 yards to look at the Joey's Memorial. At the foot of the Isle of Man's only mountain is a fitting place to commemorate the greatest TT rider, with 26 wins he is justifiably known as the King of the Mountain.

The Sound and the Calf of Man

Classification: renowned beauty spot, coastal stroll and views to Calf of Man: easy, ½ mile
OS map reference: 173667
Take the A31 from Port St Mary past Cregneash to the car park by The Sound Café.

This is undoubtedly one of the most popular scenic spot on the Island, it attracts over 100,000 visitors annually. As you drive down the views of the Calf of Man and the rocky Kitterland are particularly breath-taking. The Sound refers to the strip of sea between the islands where the current can run as fast as 8 knots. If the sea is rough the sound and sight of the waves crashing is impressive. Often too rough as there are records of at least 10 shipwrecks in the immediate vicinity. Inside the café there are information boards describing the area.

The name Calf is derived the Norse *Kalfr* meaning a small island near to a larger one. Nowadays the Calf of Man is owned by the Manx National Trust and is a wildlife sanctuary, in particular it is home to Manx shearwaters. Wardens live there part-time and there are self-catering cottages. The last permanent residents left the Calf in 1958: the family had a small child and they felt that it was wrong for her to grow up without being able to play with other children. The islet can be reached by boats from Port St Mary or Port Erin (enquiries to Manx National Heritage).

First take in the three-dimensional white Thousla Cross (modelled on

the Cross of Lorraine) – Thousla is actually the name of the even smaller islet (really just a large rock) between Kitterland and the Calf. The cross was built to commemorate the acts of bravery of men from Port St Mary in 1858 who rescued four crew members of a French schooner that came to grief on the rocks – two other members, both boys, perished in the stormy seas. The extremely rough seas meant that it was impossible to row the rescue boats from Port St Mary instead they were carried overland by relays of men.

Six years previously there was an even more tragic shipwreck. In December 1852 the Lily, whose cargo included 60 tons of gunpowder, was driven into the Sound by wind and tides. Although the captain drowned, 6 crew members were saved. The following day a large party was assembled to salvage as much of the cargo as possible. Early on in this operation smoke was seen coming from below decks; hastily a hole was cut to enable sea water to douse it. However, while this was being done the gunpowder exploded with a sound that was heard 20 miles away. The twenty five salvagers on board were blown to pieces. Many years later in America a dying man made a confession that he was partly responsible as he had been looting the ship during the previous night and had left a candle burning in the hold.

To the left, beyond the handrail, is a large flat grassed area known as The Parade – originally built up as a defensive site in pre-historic times. At the edge you may be lucky enough to see the heads of seals bobbing up and down in the water or beached on the rocks.

Further round is stone memorial to Sir Percy Cowley who helped to instigate the Manx National Trust which owns many areas of natural or historic interest, including the Calf of Man. Around here the sea has eroded deep inlets into the cliff which has exposed the folded rock strata. Follow the path round and you can see an ornate bench carved out of a single piece of wood. Finally, a little further along the path squeezes through a narrow passage which has been carved out of the cliff.

From here the adventurous can proceed further on to Spanish Head, but it entails steep climbs so you may want to head back.

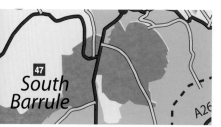

47

South Barrule

A26

A36 and A27.

South Barrule

Description: hill walk with sweeping views of whole Island, very significant pre-historic site: moderate, 1½ miles

OS map reference: 258759

There is parking at the Round Table at the junction of the

Legend has it that South Barrule is the home of the Celtic sea-god Manannan Mac Lir who would throw his cloak over the Island to hide it

in mist at times of peril. The top of this hill can often by shrouded in cloud, so it is worth checking the weather forecast before setting off. It is also said that, to further deter invaders, Manannan could make one man look like a hundred. A propitious date to climb South Barrule is the old Midsummer's Day, now Tynwald Day on 5th July. Legend has it that people would climb the hill to pay a rent of rushes to Manannan for him allowing them to use the land. He could find a use for the rushes by making a model boat and setting on the water with his enemies believing that they were seeing a fleet of a hundred ships coming to attack them.

The ascent is easy with only a small amount of moderately steep climbing towards the end. South Barrule is 1,585 feet high and is one of five 'Marliyn's' on the Isle of Man. This term was established by the hill-bagging community to describe summits that stand at least 150 metres (492 feet) above the surrounding land. The category is a jocular contrast to the more well-known classification of 'Munroes' which denotes summits of 3,000 feet or more – a homage to the famous American actress.

One start point is a wooden gate marked with the name of the hill and its altitude. Beyond this follow a path through the low heather: at a small ditch pick up the path slightly for easier walking. When this joins a wider track, which is the main footpath, bear left.

An alternative start point is a couple of hundred yards down the A27, follow the track to the left and immediately on your left is a gate and footpath sign. Follow this path all the way to the summit. The name is derived from the Norse *Warool* which means 'watch and ward' –

referring to the system by which men were appointed to watch out for any potentially hostile threat from high places right across the Island.

Behind are views of an active slate quarry surrounded by Cringle Plantation with a small reservoir adjacent. Beyond this is flat plain holding Castletown, the Langness Peninsula and Ronaldsway Airport. Jurby and Ronaldsway, which are both surrounded by extensive flat terrain and were used in World War 2, vied with each other to become the Island's civil airport. Ronaldsway was presumably chosen as it was more accessible to the capital.

From the trig point on the summit take the track on your left which heads towards a small gap in longitudinal mound a couple of hundred yards away. There is a path on the top of what is actually the outer rampart of an Iron Age fort which was occupied from possibly as early as 1000BC to 500BC. About two-thirds of the way along this path you come to a small dip, this is the edge of an inner rampart which circles the summit. The remains are lower and less pronounced than the outer as, maybe, stone was taken from this to build the bigger outer rampart.

Take the path clockwise along the top of the rampart to better appreciate the huge scale of this 3,000 year old defensive structure. The rampart is 6 feet high in places, but it is likely that it was twice this height originally. It encloses an area about 600 yards across. From here one has a 360 degree all-round view of the land and coast. Latest aerial photography techniques have been used to estimate that 120 round house sites were enclosed – not all these buildings were necessarily occupied at the same time. However, it does testify to there being a significant perceived threat from other tribes in the south of the Island, or perhaps across the Irish Sea, such that hundreds were prepared to labour to build this fort and to occupy what is a cold, windy and relatively inhospitable location. Or possibly it may have been built as a deterrent *'we're a large tribe, don't mess with us'*.

After a couple of hundred yards there is another gap in the rampart and a path that returns you to the summit. Descend the way you came.

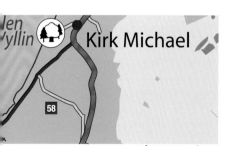

Spooyt Vane Waterfall and Keeill

Classification: woodland walk, impressive waterfall and remains of ancient keeill (chapel): easy, ½ mile
OS map reference: 308888
Follow TT course (A3) towards Kirk Michael. At Barregarrow crossroads turn left (church on the corner) and follow the minor road for a mile until you see a sign for a car park.

Take the path downhill from car park, cross a stream by wooden walkway and bear right towards a small gate a few yards in front. The

main path divides with the track on the left taking one to the remains of *Cabbal Pherick* (St Patrick's Chapel) which was built in the glade. The altar would have been at the east end of the rectangular building facing the Holy Land. Itinerant priests would have visited the site and people from nearby settlements would gather for a service that would have been held in the open at the western end. The track nearby has a plaque naming it as the Monk's Road. There are signs of a low wall enclosing the site which is likely to have also been used for burials. The chapel is named after the Irish Saint who inspired many priests to visit and preach the Christian word on the Isle of Man.

Retrace your steps and bear left down the other path towards the waterfall, which translated from Manx Gaelic means 'white spout'. There are steps and a handrail that take you to the edge of the river. This affords the best view of the waterfall which is one of the highest on the Island. It is probably significant that *Cabbal Pherick* was built close to this waterfall as it may have held special importance to those living in the area.

Return to the car park by the same route.

St Michael's Isle

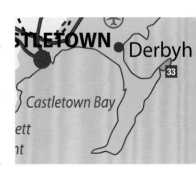

Description: undisturbed islet with historic chapel and fort, reached by causeway: easy, ½ mile.
OS map reference: 294674
Just before you enter Castletown on A5 from Douglas take the first left at the roundabout to Derbyhaven on A12. On passing the Airport perimeter turn right towards the golf course. There is a car park at the very end of this road by the hotel (which is closed) or one can drive over the causeway where there are parking spaces.

The Manx National Trust acquired St Michael's Isle in 1984 and prior to the building of the causeway it would be cut off at high tide. There are several information boards dotted around which give a comprehensive summary of the history, flora and fauna of the isle.

St Michael's Chapel was built in the 12th century by the Norse-Celtic community that lived in the area. Unlike many other Christian sites of this era it was built on a large enough scale for congregations to worship inside – the altar would have been at the far (eastern) end in the direction of the Holy Land. The many keeills of this period were much smaller permitting only the priest to pray inside while communal worship occurred outside. (It is likely that there was one such keeill on the site pre-dating the chapel). Until as recently as 150 years ago the area around the chapel was used as a burial site. Considering that it has been without a roof for several hundred years, the building is in a remarkably good state of repair: its location on a bare and windswept islet means that the stones have not been plundered by farmers as much as other ancient buildings have been.

Continue round the path by the shallow cliffs where, if you are lucky, you will see seals and cormorants.

Derby Fort was built in 16th century as part of Henry VIII's system of coastal defences – it gives the area its other name Fort Island. In 1645, during the English Civil War it was upgraded by 7th Earl Stanley to increase its ability to protect Derbyhaven which was an important natural harbour. It housed cannon which would have fired solid, non-explosive shot for a distance of around 400 yards: so it could also help defend Castletown which was the capital until the mid 19th century. The cannons collected here are from around the Island – rather than the originals of the fort. The building has also functioned as a lighthouse to guide the herring fleet safely back to harbour. It is possible that this was a fortified site in the mid-13th century. The Battle of Ronaldsway was fought across Derbyhaven Bay in 1275 when the Scottish King Alexander III sent soldiers over to quell rebellious Manx who were

threatening law and order on the Island which had been recently acquired by Scotland.

Owing to its sheltered location Derbyhaven was actually the leading port on the Island in the 17th century with a considerable fleet of fishing boats. To save boats having to navigate round the tide-swept Dreswick Point on Langness a track existed to haul boats across the short strip of land to Castletown Bay. The track was built in the 13th century by the Norse King Ronald and it became known as *Ronaldswath* or *Ronaldsway*.

After circling the fort continue along the path with Derbyhaven Bay on your right and Castletown in the distance. As you pass the chapel on your left you will see a low ridge and numerous tussocky clumps of grass which denote the graves and the wall that enclosed them.

The Sugarloaf and Anvil

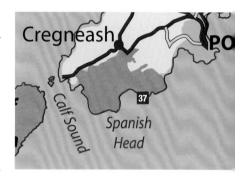

Description: countryside and cliff walk, Island's most dramatic coastline feature: easy to moderate, 1¾ miles
OS map reference: 202675
Drive into Port St Mary and follow the road round to the right where going straight on is prohibited (one-way system). After a couple of hundred yards bear right into Fistard Road. Continue past a left turn (Perwick Road) and a right turn. The road bends then widens: here is a good place to park.

Continue walking down this road, it becomes steep as it crosses over a small river flowing into Perwick Bay. Ignore the sharp turn on the right and continue forward. The road winds uphill following the blue Coastal Footpath waymarker – a sign indicates the road is unsuitable for motor vehicles.

Views of a patchwork of green pastureland and yellow gorse open up in front and behind one can easily make out Perwick Bay, Port St Mary, Castletown and Langness with its white lighthouse. On the right by a derelict barn (known locally as the Red Shed) is a plaque in the wall marking where Ned Maddrell, the last native Manx Gaelic speaker, would sit and chat with his friends. Ned was somewhat a celebrity. When Irish Taoiseach Éamon de Valera visited the Island in the late 1940s he called upon Ned personally. De Valera was a keen advocate of Irish Gaelic and was angered that the Manx Government was doing little to preserve the Island's old language. Ned's death on 27th December 1974 marked the passing of the last native speaker: however, he left a legacy of interest in the language and it is recorded that over a thousand now speak it with some fluency.

As the tarmac road ends cross over the stile by a Coastal Footpath

sigh onto a grassed farm track. Ignore the public footpath sign and keep following the route indicated by the blue waymarkers. Another stile and blue sign leads to a chequerboard of dry stone walls, lined by bracken in the summer, marking out the path and field boundaries. A waymarker indicates the path turns right uphill towards a gate. Bear left at the sign for The Chasms. Climb towards another stile and blue sign: continue forwards for another ten yards.

Here the most breath-taking cliff scenery is on your left, with the rocky promontory of the Anvil and the adjacent isolated stack known as the Sugar Loaf. From the sea it looks like an anvil but, some do say, from above it resembles a church pulpit. This is home to hundreds of sea birds including guillemots, kittiwakes, fulmars and the occasional puffin – so it well worth having a pair of binoculars with you. Few have climbed the Sugar Loaf and access is only by sea. The first recorded ascent was in 1933 by Dr Kelly who actually swam out to it in shorts and plimsolls and reached the top without ropes or any other climbing equipment.

Return by following the same path and on a clear day you should be able to see far north to the summit of Snaefell with its twin masts.

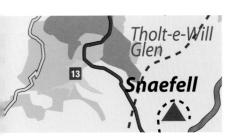

Sulby Reservoir

Description: walk round Island's largest reservoir in rugged upland countryside: easy, 1mile
OS map reference: 374890
Take the Mountain Road (A18) to the Bungalow and follow A14 signposted Sulby. After 2½ miles there is a left turn to a car park.

Sulby Reservoir is the largest and most recently constructed reservoir on the Island. It was completed in 1982 and involved building a dam across the Sulby River whose source is close to Hailwood Heights (the highest part of the TT Course) and is the Island's longest river at 11 miles. The capacity of the reservoir is 10 billion gallons and is 80 feet deep: it supplies almost all of the west and north of the Island. It is, arguably, also the most scenic reservoir with uplifting views of several hill summits and the extensive Tholt-e-will Plantation. The site is also designated as a Dark Sky Discovery Area.

There are two very gentle walks: one slightly longer to the left of the car park, the other across the dam itself. The longer path starts by leaving the car park either by the wooden gate or stile and following the tarmac track. This turns into an even grass path which might be slightly muddy in certain places if it has been raining recently. Across the water one can see derelict farm buildings which were probably vacated long before the valley was flooded. Occasionally a stone wall tumbles down the hillside and stops abruptly by the path. On this stretch you will encounter both types of gorse that grow on the Island. The lower lying bush which only flowers in the summer is a native plant which colonised the Island over ten thousand years ago when the last Ice Age came to an end. The taller variety which flowers all year round is European gorse which was introduced about four hundred years ago as it has good burning qualities for domestic fires.

Grass extends almost down to the shore: an excellent spot for a picnic and a place to chill your drinks. As it nears the pipe and bridge crossing the river the path peters out. For those interested in more adventure the path continues over the river and round the reservoir, but it is quite a challenging 4 mile walk up to Druidale Farm. Otherwise turn round here and return to the car park.

The shorter route starts on the dam where an information board

describes several other walks in the vicinity. Looking to the right one can appreciate the extent of the earth moving required to build the dam – the embankment is over 200 feet high. The tarmac track bears right past a storage building and ends at a short descent down to the reservoir shore. It is possible to pick ones way across the rocks to come closer to the inlet which is surrounded by trees. This is another peaceful spot for a picnic. Return to the car park the way you came.

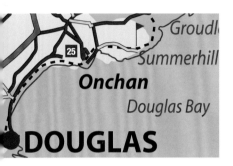

Summerhill Glen

Description: woodland walk by river with many curiosities, floodlit at night: easy to moderate, ¾ mile
OS map reference: 394775
Park at the northern end of Douglas Promenade and walk 200 yards up Summerhill Road to find a red brick archway which is the lower entrance. (Alternatively, one can park on Victoria Road, just down from the junction with Glencrutchery Road, for the upper entrance).

Summerhill Glen is filled with streams and footpaths to explore and a vast array of flora and fauna. It is a gem of natural beauty close to the centre of Douglas. At night times it has a dramatic lighting display (it is illuminated from August through to the end of December). The glen was developed in 1932-1933 by 187 young men aged between 18 and 22 on a 'work for the workless' scheme.

Follow the steps up through the archway into an ornamental garden. Once you are through another archway the path is tarmac'd and you can hear the stream rushing past. There are a number of interesting artefacts to spot on the walk. Seats have been created from old oil drums and lampshades are made from dozens of plastic water bottles. At the bottom of the trunks of many trees you will see little fairy doors, each individually painted and named.

Keep going on the main route, there are paths to the right which will be used on the way back. The path eventually leaves the glen at Victoria Avenue. Turn round here and walk back downhill. Take the first smaller path on the left using the footbridge so the river is on your right. This path lifts one just out of the wood so you can see open fields on your left. You meet a set of concrete steps on the left which descend to the main path or carry on straight ahead for the higher level route. This path eventually winds its way downhill to return to the riverside route.

As you descend the concrete steps there is a small grassed area on the right with two cannons pointing out over Douglas Bay.

Tholt-y-Will Glen

Description: woodland walk, steepling views down Sulby valley, delightful waterfall: easy to moderate, 1½ miles.
OS Map Reference: 378897
Take the A14 either from the Mountain Road (A18) at the Bungalow or from the A3 from Sulby crossroads. There is a car park opposite the tea rooms at Tholt-y-Will.

The name Tholt-y-Will is derived from *Tolta-yn-wooliae* which is Celtic for 'hill of the cattlefold'. Cross the road and walk over the grass to the wooden gate and bridge across the river to enter the glen. The Sulby River is the longest river on the Island at just over 11 miles. It rises at the top of the valley between Snaefell and Beinn-y-Phott and flows into Sulby Reservoir and then heads to Ramsey. It is fed by a couple of tributaries that rise in the glen. The river's flow is regulated by the reservoir so, unless it is full and there is an overflow, the river is not as awesome a sight as it might be.

This became the first National Glen when it was purchased from the Manx Electric Railway Company by the Forestry Board in 1952. The MER had acquired the land 30 years earlier as an attraction to encourage visitors to use the Snaefell Mountain Railway, which was one of the principal ways of reaching it. At the height of the tourism boom in the 1890s there was an hotel, tearooms and a 'museum of Manx curiosities'.

There used to be a circular path around the glen. However, at the time of writing one arm of the path had been closed 'awaiting repairs' (locals say that that there are no plans for this). The other section of the path is easily navigable and takes in the waterfall.

Follow the cinder track which passes a glorious lily pond in the garden on the right of the fence. The first stretch passes through the

mixed deciduous and evergreen woodland with serried ranks of ferns stretching up the slope. Hairpin left when you reach the fence that closes off the unsafe route. The grassed path climbs gently, you notice storm-felled trees on your right. As you climb the sound of the rushing Sulby River diminishes to be replaced by silence or the occasional birdsong. On your left dramatic views of Sulby valley open up. At a gap in the low wall hairpin right gently uphill rather than continuing straight on. The gradient picks up but there is a flight of stairs to help the ascent. When you reach an old fence follow the path right as it levels off and the sound of rushing water returns.

Steps lead down towards the river and here one can appreciate the mixed tree species that were planted by the Victorians to boost the appeal of the glen as a tourist attraction. The tall pines that you have been walking through were generally planted in the mid-20th century. On the left there is a towering, but relatively slim, waterfall dropping into a crystal clear plunge pool. Cross the river and climb using the concrete steps. Pause to get close to the multi-coloured mosses and ferns that cling to the vertical rock walls – it has the feel of a deep pile carpet and results from the continual moist atmosphere provided by the waterfall.

As you climb you encounter the fence that closes the top of route that is 'awaiting repair'. One can follow the short, steep zig-zag path further until it reaches the main road. After the first hairpin there is an amazing view of the Sulby valley through the trees, but after that there are no notable features along the way. Otherwise turn round and retrace your steps to the car park.

Tynwald Hill and Cooill y Ree Gardens

Description: place of national significance, re-creation of Manx woodlands through time: easy, ½ mile
OS map reference: 278820
There is parking by the side of the road at Tynwald green in St John's

This walk dramatises the history of the Isle of Man over several millennia. Tynwald Hill is the site of the island's annual open air Parliament whose origins date back to 979AD. Cooill y Ree Garden recreates a snapshot of the landscape that early settlers on the island might have encountered.

Start at the door of St John's Church. The chapel of St John was first referred to in 1557, but it was likely that there was a keeill (small chapel) on the same site over 1,000 years ago. The previous chapel was demolished and the current one built in 1849. On the Manx National Day (5th July) the Members of Tynwald and other officials gather for a service in St John's. This is a formal sitting of the Island's parliament and the only one in the world to take place in a Christian church. To permit Members who are non-Christians to attend proceedings the area where they sit is not consecrated.

Following the service, the dignitaries walk down the 100 yard long gravelled processional way, which is covered by freshly cut rushes (to appease the Celtic sea god Manannan), towards Tynwald Hill. This is known as Cronk y Keeillown. The hill is believed to have been made in the 13th century from soil taken from each of the 17 parishes, so that each of the local chieftains could feel that they were on home ground. There are suggestions that the hill may have originally been a Bronze Age burial mound (perhaps dating to 2000BC).

The annual open air assembly of officials in Norse times was known as Thing vollr – thing being an assembly and vollr a field – hence the name Tynwald arises. Tynwald was established by the recently arrived Vikings during which disputes were settled and new 'laws' were proclaimed to the assembled population. Nowadays, there is a reading, in English and Manx, of the summary of all new legislation that has been passed in the previous 12 months. Residents are allowed to petition Tynwald to have new laws considered or wrongs redressed.

The four tiers of Tynwald Hill are occupied by officials of different seniority and significance during the open air ceremony. The Lieutenant Governor (the UK monarch's representative on the Island) and the Bishop sit on the top tier. The next tier is occupied by the Deemsters (equivalent to Judges in UK). On the third tier sit the twenty four Members of the House of Keys (equivalent to UK MP's). On the final tier the four Coroners and Captains of the 17 parishes are seated. Thus, all the Island's key officials are assembled in plain view of the public.

The Giant's Grave, a Bronze Age burial mound is less than 30 yards north of the Hill, is dated several centuries BC.

Cross the road to the viewing platform looking over Cooill y Ree which was opened in 2001. The name is Manx for Nook of the King. The main path, which runs westwards, is known as the Avenue of Time and is intended to depict elements of the landscape of the Isle of Man from prehistoric times whereas the view east back to the church represents the last thousand years.

Follow the track downwards to reach the main level of the park. Follow the raised walkway through vegetation representing thickets which were gradually cleared for farming during the early settlement of the Island from about 8,000 years ago. On the left is a modern interpretation of a Viking longsword, chair and standing stone. Proceed along the path: to represent the Island becoming more intensely managed the landscaping becomes more formalised with an avenue of trees and shrubs. The tree species become more exotic representing the increasing international influences on the Isle of Man. The path ends at the Circle of Infinity which represents the continuation of life on the Island.

Windy Corner (Slieau Lhost)

Description: the shortest walk to a significant hill summit, panoramic views of Douglas and Laxey: easy to moderate, ½ mile.
OS map reference: 391845
There is a pulling in place on the Mountain Road (A18) at Windy Corner by the Marshal's hut.

The summit at Windy Corner is known as *Slieau Lhost* which translates from Manx Gaelic as 'burnt fell', is 445 metres (1460 feet) – although the ascent from the road is only 70 metres. Windy Corner is aptly named as winds rush up the Baldwin valley over the brow of the hill and down towards Laxey. Although it is a gentle curve on the TT Course, the gusty winds can make it hazardous for riders.

Proceed through the gate to right of cattle grid then towards the stone wall into which slate steps have been fixed. Pick your route carefully as the first 50 yards can be a little boggy if it has rained recently. The path over grass and heather is clearly visible snaking up the hill. A large cairn marks the top, there is a walled enclosure built into it to give shelter to any sheep that are brave enough to venture up here. The cairn is called *Cairn Gerjoil* (The Devil's Cairn) and is possibly a Bronze Age burial site (1500 – 800BC).

This summit affords great views north and east (to your left) of rolling pastureland of Glen Roy in the direction of Laxey and the plantations around the Creg ny Baa Back Road. On the right Douglas and its Bay are laid out in the distance. On a clear day you will be able to see the

Lake District hills to the east across the Irish Sea.

Folklore has it that on Easter Sunday anyone who went up to the top of a high hill to watch sunrise would see the sun bow 2 or 3 times as if in adoration to the risen Saviour. As there is an unobstructed view due east this would be as good a place as any to test this lore.

As the summit is easily accessible and one of the most easterly, and therefore visible from England (in good weather), it has been used as for the site of a beacon to celebrate the Queen's Diamond Jubilee celebrations (2012) and her 90th birthday (2016). It joined in with other beacons lit across the British Isles.

Although it is well-concealed, the Slieau Lhost shooting range is only a few hundred yards away to the south. It is a civilian shooting range, owned and used by Peveril Rifle Club. It has as 50 and 25 metres ranges, used for full bore rifle, practical pistol, and muzzle loaders. If the range is in use, and the wind is from the south, you might hear gun fire although I never have.

The route down is the same as the route up.